(Continued)

CHANGING TEACHING, CHANGING SCHOOLS

Bringing Early Childhood Practice into Public Education

CASE STUDIES FROM THE KINDERGARTEN

Frances O'Connell Rust

FOREWORD BY ROLAND S. BARTH

TEACHERS COLLEGE PRESS

Teachers College, Columbia University
New York and London

Published by Teachers College Press, 1234 Amsterdam Avenue
New York, New York

Library of Congress Cataloging-in-Publication Data

Rust, Frances O'Connell.
  Changing teaching, changing schools : bringing early childhood
practice into public education : case studies from the kindergarten /
Frances O'Connell Rust ; foreword by Roland S. Barth.
  p.   cm. — (Early childhood education series)
  Includes bibliographical references and index.
  ISBN 0–8077–3286–9. — ISBN 0–8077–3285–0 (pbk.)
  1. Early childhood education—United States.   2. Kindergarten—
United States—Case studies.   3. Educational change—United States.
I. Title.   II. Series.
LB1139.25R87   1993
372.21—dc20   93-17378

ISBN 0–8077–3285–0 (pbk.)
ISBN 0–8077–3286–9

Printed on acid-free paper
Manufactured in the United States of America

99 98 97 96 95 94 93   7 6 5 4 3 2 1

For Lang, Ned, and Susanne
with love and thanks for your patience and good humor

Contents

Part III: LOOKING AHEAD

Foreword

As the beginning principal of an elementary school, I arrived to find a printed faculty directory organized in what appeared to be reverse order: The sixth grade teachers were listed at the top; the kindergarten teachers at the bottom. Peculiar, I thought. Chronological order, whether by grade level or ages of children, would suggest otherwise. So I "corrected" the directory, listing the kindergarten teachers first. With the repercussions that followed began my painful education about the relationship between early childhood education and what is known as "elementary education."

This provocative little volume dramatically extends that education. It reveals just how embedded in the thinking and practice of parents, administrators, board members, and teachers of older children are misleading and pejorative stereotypes about early childhood education. And it reveals in vivid detail the nature and extent of the impediments advocates of kindergarten face as they attempt to bring what they know to be good education for youngsters into the elementary schoolhouse.

Early childhood education plays a peripheral role in most schools. More typically, the kindergarten is a school-within-a-school, an unwanted appendage, safely hidden away in the basement, somehow lacking rigor, legitimacy, and intellectual substance. And somehow embarrassing to the real school. There is not a good fit between these two cultures. The problem is sometimes stated as: How do we integrate the kindergarten into the regular school? Occasionally the question is upgraded to: How do we make kindergarten, kindergartners, and kindergarten teachers first class citizens of this school?

But Frances Rust poses a more daring—some would say outrageous—question: How do we make deliberate use of the art form of early childhood education as a major and enlightened force in reforming elementary schools? Kindergartners should not accommodate, thereby losing their childhood. Rather, teachers and students in older classes should adapt so they may find themselves as voracious learners.

As a university teacher, I begin one large, three-hour class by announcing that, henceforth, I will talk no more than fifteen minutes each period. "What are we going to do the other two and three quarter hours?" Exactly. What are *we* going to do? I learned as an elementary school teacher that after about fifteen minutes of me the kids would hang from the lights. So do older kids. So do adults—only we do it more politely.

For me then, good education, at whatever level, is more akin to the best practice of the early childhood model than to, say, the best didactic instruction in the university. Cooperation, playfulness, risk taking, whimsy, hands-on experiences, feelings accompanied by laughter or tears, developmentally appropriate activities, student-centeredness, joy, milk and cookies—these are the conditions which cause the learning curves of all human beings to soar. This is why Robert Fulgham touched such an astonishing chord in all of us with "All I ever needed to know I learned in kindergarten." And this is why, as principal, my rule of thumb when hiring a new teacher was: always hire a teacher of younger children for a position working with older children. I never failed to improve instruction.

These characteristics of early childhood education are desperately needed in transforming and restructuring the dominant school culture from a transmission of knowledge model with a short memory, to an experience-based model with a far longer memory. Early childhood programs have demonstrated, through Head Start for instance, that they can bring renewal, energy, and learning to young children and relief and insights to their working parents. It may just be that early childhood education can bring renewal, relief, and vision to elementary schools as well.

The road will continue to be bumpy, contentious, and uncharted, for early childhood education holds a mirror to conventional practice. The image revealed is often not a laudatory one, as the two perplexing case studies which follow reveal. The presence under the same roof of a discrepant way of thinking about promoting learning in young people uncovers all the warts attendant to important school issues: pedagogy, curriculum, staff development, leadership, legitimacy, purpose.

Herein is a consideration of the relationship of early childhood education to the elementary school. What follows is a heady mix of rich description coupled with thoughtful analysis. "Early childhood practice has the power to transform the elementary school," says Rust. I agree. Will we have the courage to unlock, celebrate, and make wise use of this power? Read on!

Roland S. Barth
Harvard University

Preface

Increasingly, programs for young children are being adopted by school systems around the country. While the appropriateness of their being in the schools is a matter of considerable debate, the fact is they are there. Their adoption by the schools has had profound implications for early childhood and elementary educators as well as for school administrators, policy-makers, parents, and communities. It has occasioned broad-based and searching review and reconsideration of such basic issues as curriculum, instruction, staffing, licensing, services, finances, and equity. Few, however, are focusing on how best to incorporate early childhood programs into the schools and on the impact of their adoption on schools and on the field of early childhood itself. This book is designed to address these important issues by focusing specifically on cases of early childhood programs being initiated in schools.

In 1984, I completed a case study of a school district's effort to initiate an all-day kindergarten program. The outcome of that effort was an extended morning kindergarten—an additional hour of kindergarten that lengthened the school day from 11:15 to 12:15. Now, almost 10 years later, the extended morning kindergarten is thriving; there is no all-day kindergarten program, and it is unlikely that there will be one any time soon. To some in the district, the outcome was a success because they got the longer day that they wanted; to others, the outcome was a failure because they had set out to initiate all-day kindergarten and they ended up only slightly closer to their goal than they were when they began. For me, the researcher, the outcome was unimportant in comparison to the knowledge I gained about the process of change and about the problems of integrating early childhood programs into the schools.

Since 1984, I have been involved as a consultant in a number of other efforts to initiate all-day kindergarten programs. Each has taught me more about the change process. Each has reconfirmed for me the lessons I learned about perceptions of early childhood education among school people, parents, and communities: Few understand how very different early childhood education is from elementary education, and few are prepared for the emotion-laden battles that frequently accompany the adoption of early childhood programs by schools.

From these experiences, I have learned that it is important to enter into the change process prepared, knowing what the critical issues are likely to be, knowing some of the "do's" and "don'ts" that research on change in schools has yielded over the past 20 years, and knowing that change takes time. I have learned that change is not an isolated event in schools. While many change efforts are likely to be underway at any one time even in the smallest school systems, there are also a myriad of day-to-day activities that take time, energy, and management. Hence, neither administrators nor teachers have the luxury to attend soley to the guidance of an innovation. Change, then, is a social process that engages many—some a lot of the time and closely, some occasionally and peripherally. I have learned that the process of change is often slow, its outcome, uncertain. The more substantive the change, the more complex the change process is likely to be.

Finally, I have learned that innovations involving early childhood education are fraught with difficulty: Many who are not early childhood educators think preparing an educational program for young children is easy, and hence bringing early childhood into the schools should be fairly straightforward and simple; many who are early childhood educators are unaware of what Sarason (1982) terms "the regularities" of schooling, those habitual patterns of operation that are likely to interfere with developmentally appropriate practice for young children; and many early childhood educators are not accustomed to educating adults about early childhood practice.

This book is designed to speak to early childhood educators and other change agents introducing new programs and to those who are interested in adopting early childhood programs. It is for parents, teachers, administrators, school board members, and other policy-makers. Its general focus is the process of change in schools; its specific focus is the process of change that accompanies the adoption of early childhood programs in schools.

The book is constructed around two case studies of all-day kindergarten initiatives. I have chosen to use case studies because, like all good stories, they enable one to get beneath the surface, offering opportunity for reflection and analysis from multiple perspectives. All-day kindergarten is the focus of these case studies because I believe that it encompasses most of the critical issues that relate to early childhood and the schools—issues of time, care, learning, and good education. In many ways, kindergarten is the test case for early childhood practice in the schools: Kindergarten has been accepted as part of the mainstream of the elementary school; it is familiar. Efforts to change it raise questions. Suggestions that curriculum and teaching in the primary grades might be improved by the infusion of those early childhood practices that have been the hallmark of the kindergarten cause significant discomfort, even alarm. Case studies from the kindergarten that focus on the change process can help us to understand the issues involved in bringing this and other early childhood programs into the schools as well as provide us with insight about how to plan for, guide, and support these initiatives.

The book is divided into three parts. Part I is an overview of the issues related to early childhood education and educational change. Chapter 1 focuses on kindergarten and its fit within the framework of elementary education. Chapter 2 provides a review of research on change and innovation in schools, with particular emphasis on issues related to bringing early childhood programs into the schools.

Part II presents the cases from the field. It begins in Chapter 3 with a description and rationale of the field research methods that I used to develop the case studies. Chapters 4 and 5 cover two case studies of efforts to initiate all-day kindergarten programs. Both are composites of initiatives in which I was involved. The first is based on the study I completed for my dissertation (Rust, 1984). The second is based on my work as a consultant to school systems developing all-day kindergarten programs. Chapter 6 provides an analysis of these two cases and draws conclusions about the initiation, implementation, and management of early childhood programs in schools.

Part III describes the challenges that face early childhood change agents as they attempt to establish early childhood programs in the schools, and it considers the impact of the programs' adoption on the schools and on the field of early childhood itself.

There is genuine concern among early childhood educators that with the movement of early childhood programs into the schools and the concomitant pressure on young children for early academic achievement, we are witnessing the erosion of childhood (Elkind, 1981; Winn, 1983). It seems imperative that we study not only how young children fare in these programs but also whether and how those qualities that have made early childhood education a special and significant force in the lives of countless children can survive and flourish in a new territory—the public school.

Part I

THE ISSUES

CHAPTER 1

Early Childhood Education, the Kindergarten, and Schools: Is There a Fit?

In the past 30 years, educational programs for young children have multiplied significantly, reaching children at all socio-economic levels (Chovinsky, 1982). These programs are remarkable for their diversity (Caldwell, 1991; Grubb, 1991; Hauser-Cram, Pierson, Walker, & Tivnan, 1991): They range from programs for infants and toddlers to traditional nursery schools. They can last only an hour or two or for the whole day. Some are morning programs; some are afternoon programs; some programs are open around the clock and every day of the week. Some are housed in church basements; others operate from their own buildings. Some are funded solely by parents; some receive federal, state, and/or local government funding. Some are church related. Many are privately sponsored. Many combine both child care and education—"educare," as Caldwell (1989) describes it, in which distinctions between child care and early education do not exist. "Today," write Rust and Williams (1989),

> high-quality child care assumes the provision of educational opportunities across the age range served. Programs originally designed as educational have been expanded to include important elements of care, that is, provision of nutritional and social services, and extended or full-day options. (p. viii)

With the exception of kindergarten, early childhood programs have not been in the mainstream of schooling. There are a number of reasons for this.

1. Economic factors and family patterns that have supported keeping children at home during their early years (Spodek, 1988)
2. Distinctions in the public mind between early childhood education and regular schooling (Campbell, 1987; Shanker, 1987)
3. Profound differences in the educational philosophies of elementary and early childhood professionals (Campbell, 1987; Goffin, 1989; Hauser-Cram et al., 1991; Moore, 1987)

The advent of Head Start in the mid-1960s together with the work of Benjamin Bloom (1964), Jerome Bruner (1960), Jean Piaget (1950) and others, however, began a significant shift in perceptions about early childhood education.

Now, almost 30 years later, the advantages of early education, particularly for children of poverty, are generally acknowledged (Caruso & Detterman, 1982; Clark, 1984; Jarvis & Molnar, 1986; Schultz & Lombardi, 1989; Schweinhart, Weikart, & Larner, 1986). While the general benefits of early education are touted, the gradual movement of early childhood programs into public schools has not been so readily accepted. The debate about the length of the kindergarten day is a case in point, for it epitomizes the controversy surrounding early childhood programs in schools.

KINDERGARTEN: THEN AND NOW

Until recently, kindergarten was the first school experience for most young children: It served as a bridge between home and school and between early childhood education and the primary school (Stegelin, 1992). Thus, curriculum and instruction in the kindergarten were qualitatively different from those of the rest of the elementary school—even the first grade. In the kindergarten, the focus was the "whole child." There was time for play, and play was understood to be the child's work. Kindergarten teachers planned activities to encourage children's exploration of their environment and interaction with one another. Readiness for school came as a by-product of the kindergarten experience. Assessment was geared toward understanding the individual child (Perrone, 1990).

Kindergartens have changed. "In many ways," write Goffin and Stegelin (1992), "kindergarten education has become the new battleground for resolution of what constitutes developmentally appropriate practice within the public school early primary setting" (p. xii). Where once there was a sense of freedom with regard to the curriculum, now there is pressure on parents and early childhood teachers to make sure that children are ready for school even before they get there. Screening for kindergarten is commonplace, and testing of kindergartners is almost routine. To a large extent, assessment drives the kindergarten curriculum (Elkind, 1991; Kamii, 1990).

In recent years, the traditional kindergarten curriculum has been expanded to include instruction in reading, math, and many of the subject areas taught in the elementary grades. However, the length of the kindergarten has not been extended. The result has been a rushed, even pressured, experience for both children and teachers as more material is packed into a short day. There is less time for play and socialization—the traditional focus of kindergarten—and increased emphasis on academic work (Karweit, 1988; Silvern, 1988).

These changes came gradually and were accomplished with little fanfare. It was not until the early 1980s, when the press for all-day kindergarten and programs for four-year-olds in the schools became so widespread, that early childhood educators' concerns about developmentally inappropriate practice (Elkind, 1986) and fears about its effects on children's future success in learning (Suransky, 1982) began to draw attention. Until that time, it seems as if kindergarten occupied a special place in elementary schools, a place where it was assumed that a different kind of teaching and a different set of expectations about curriculum and learning prevailed.

DEVELOPMENTALLY APPROPRIATE PRACTICE

The hallmark of the kindergarten and, really, of all good early childhood education has been the child-centered, nurturant quality of these settings. Good early childhood practice is developmentally appropriate.

The concept of developmental appropriateness has "two dimensions: age appropriateness and individual appropriateness" (National Association for the Education of Young Children, 1986, p. 5). Age appropriateness has to do with matching curriculum and instruction to the developmental level (physical, social, emotional, and cognitive) of the children being served. Individual appropriateness has to do with responsiveness to the unique modes of learning and capabilities of each child in a program. Developmentally appropriate practice in early childhood and kindergarten programs is reflected in curriculum, adult–child interaction, relations between the home and the school, and assessment strategies. "The aim of developmental education," writes Elkind (1991), is "to produce creative, critical thinkers. This is not achieved by teaching children and adolescents thinking skills, but rather by creating developmentally appropriate learning environments that will encourage and challenge the child's emerging mental abilities" (p. 8).

Developmentally appropriate learning environments are, as Fromberg (1989) suggests, constructivist in intent; that is, it is assumed that individuals actively construct knowledge and that, in doing so, they are using higher-order thinking skills. The constructivist position, which has emerged from Piaget's (1950) studies of children's thinking, holds that children are actively engaged in making meaning and building understandings of the world. In learning environments that are guided by a constructivist view of children's thinking, we would expect to see children actively learning and, in the process, developing a strong sense of independence and autonomy. In such settings, we would expect teachers to engage in hands-on, interactive activity such as that described by Fromberg (1987, 1989) and Katz and Chard (1989). We would anticipate their implementing curricula for the children that are "localized" (Elkind, 1991, p. 12) or "familiar," as Bowman (1991, p. 27) describes it. Curriculum in such settings, Katz (1991) suggests, is "related to the young child's life and surround" (p. 62). Workbooks and ditto sheets are inappropriate in early childhood settings; so, too, is whole group instruction. Instead, we would expect to see a variety of types of group work and cooperative and independent projects in which the focus is on dialogue, sharing, and the development of voice. The thrust of such teaching, Fromberg (1987, 1989), Elkind (1991), Kamii (1990), and others note, is toward understanding, problem-solving, and independent thinking, rather than toward the mastery of skills out of context. Furthermore, since early childhood education places great value on multiculturalism and pluralism, we would expect to see activities that heighten children's awareness of their own cultural backgrounds as well as of the diversity of perspectives that inform most problems. Looking at the overall ethos of such schools, we would expect to find adaptive environments that are sensitive to the individual needs of children and to their family and cultural backgrounds (Fromberg, 1989; Heath, 1983; Suransky, 1982), rather than schools molding children to fit their structures.

Beckner and others (1979), Campbell (1987), Hiebert (1988), and Hilliard (1991) found the attitudes and skills of teachers in early childhood programs to be critically important in children's performance. Teachers of young children should be thoroughly grounded in child development as well as in early childhood pedagogy (Elkind, 1991; Spodek, 1991). Hilliard (1991) stresses the early childhood teacher's importance when he suggests that new teachers "have an opportunity to observe someone being successful with the types of students who are most likely to fail in school, such as low-income children and racial minority groups" (p. 205).

Evaluation is a critical element in planning and implementing developmentally appropriate programs (Bredekamp & Shepard, 1989; Kamii, 1990; NAEYC, 1988; Shepard & Smith, 1988). Both formal assessments such as standardized tests and informal assessments such as observations, performance samples, and anecdotal records can provide a comprehensive picture of a particular child's capabilities. With young children, evaluation should be designed and used not to try to fit children to existing programs but to "improve services to children and to ensure that children benefit from their educational experience" (NAEYC, 1988, p. 44).

In developmentally appropriate early childhood programs, partnership between teachers and families in children's education is axiomatic to a program's viability. Rather than being considered a downward articulation of the elementary school, early childhood education is best considered as an extension of family and community (Elkind, 1986). As the work of Suransky (1982), Heath (1983), Comer (1980, 1989), and others (e.g., Hauser-Cram et al., 1991; Schorr, 1988, 1989; Silvern, 1988) illustrates, early childhood programs that create an effective synthesis of school, family, and culture can be of profound importance in helping children to realize their intellectual and social potential. This is true regardless of a child's socio-economic status. Parent involvement benefits everyone: Children see that school is important and are motivated to succeed (Hauser-Cram et al., 1991). Parents often gain in self-confidence as well as develop understanding of their children and the school program (Cummins, 1986; Comer, 1989). Schools inevitably benefit because of high motivation on the part of students, high commitment from parents, and greater understanding among teachers of the families and communities with which they are working (Comer, 1989; Zigler, 1991).

Early childhood and all-day kindergarten programs that incorporate these developmentally appropriate practices in curriculum design, adult–child interactions, relationships between home and school, and assessment have been shown to have positive long-term carryover in children's attitudes toward school and society (Cotton & Conklin, 1989; Schweinhart, Weikart, & Larner, 1986).

THE MOVEMENT TOWARD ALL-DAY KINDERGARTEN

Lengthening the kindergarten day can have far-reaching effects on a school community (Hills, 1985; Rust, 1984). It is, as Hills (1985) suggests, "tinkering of consequence" (p. 10). Curriculum, instruction, staffing, program management, evaluation, home–school interactions, school–community relations—all are affected; however, despite these potential problems, school districts are increasingly moving toward all-day kindergarten. This movement has been fueled by a variety of economic, political, and social conditions impinging on families and schools (Hills, 1985; Kagan & Zigler, 1987; Karweit, 1988; Oelerich, 1979; Peskin, 1988).

Pressures for Change

Among the many social issues cited as reasons for implementing all-day kindergarten programs are a growing need for child care (Edelman, 1989; Galinsky, 1991; Magid, 1989), the need for more opportunity for socialization among young children, and a demand for more academically challenging programs (Naron, 1981). Having few alternatives, parents have turned for support to the schools (Association for Supervision and Curriculum Development, 1988; Kagan & Zigler, 1987; Katz, 1987). And the schools have responded in a variety of ways, including all-day kindergarten, thereby, according to Kagan and Zigler (1987), "accelerating the debate regarding their role in caring for and educating young children" (p. xiv).

Widespread belief in the value and importance of early childhood education is another factor that has fueled the all-day kindergarten movement (Katz, 1987; Peskin, 1988; Zigler, 1987). In the effort to enhance student achievement, the remarkable outcomes of publicly funded early childhood programs such as Head Start (Lazar & Darlington, 1982), the Perry Preschool Project (Berrueta-Clement, Schweinhart, Barnett, Epstein, & Weikart, 1984), and the Brookline Early Education Program (Hauser-Cram et al., 1991) have caught the attention of many. And it is the success of these programs, in particular the long-term academic gains made by the low socio-economic status children who have participated in them, that has spurred current efforts to bring early childhood education into schools, thereby making it available to all children (Weikart, 1987; Zigler, 1987). The assumption at work here is that there are also advantages to early childhood education for middle-class children. Little, however, is known about this issue (Nieman & Gastright, 1981; Olsen & Zigler, 1989; Peskin, 1988). Caldwell (1991) calls the lack of research on the effects of early childhood education on middle-class children "the equivalent of a metaphorical black hole in our cosmos of data on the effects of early experience" (p. 75).

There are practical reasons, too, for the movement to all-day kindergarten. These include excess classroom space and a high number of teacher layoffs—an outgrowth of declining enrollments nationwide; the need to reduce transportation costs—a by-product of the double busing run required by most half-day programs; and the desirability of closing and consolidating schools (Hills, 1985; Katz, 1987; Peskin, 1988).

Program Structure and Curriculum

There are a variety of models for lengthening the kindergarten day. These include

- Extended day programs: the addition of an hour to a half-day schedule
- All-day/alternate day programs: Children come to school for a full day every other day. The fifth day is used for planning
- Call-back programs: Some children remain in school all day several days a week. These programs are generally used for remediation
- All-day/every day

There is no standardized curriculum for all-day kindergarten. Typical patterns for creating all-day kindergartens have been (1) to balloon traditional half-day programs (oriented to socialization) to fill the longer time period, thus creating a less hurried day and giving children more time for exploration, and (2) to transfer an elementary school curriculum (with emphasis on early reading and math) and apply it to the kindergarten population. Early childhood educators such as Fromberg (1987), Jarvis and Molnar (1986), and Katz and Chard (1989) advocate developmentally appropriate curricula that are child-centered and rich in hands-on, interactive activities designed to promote problem-solving and independent thinking. There is great concern among early childhood educators that many all-day kindergartens have adopted the academic orientation of the elementary school and that the kindergarten has, for all intents and purposes, become what Katz (1987) describes as a "'pushed-down' first grade" (p. 157). This is a result, writes Peskin (1988) of the fact that "too often the decision to have all-day kindergarten is made by administrators who have not sought counsel from early childhood educators before or after making the decision" (p. 5).

Effects

While it has been possible to assess the effectiveness of various federal and state sponsored early childhood programs such as Head Start, the research on the effects of all-day kindergarten is problematic mostly because there is no standard all-day kindergarten curriculum or program on which to base comparisons.

It is estimated that 40–45% of all five-year-olds today attend full-day kindergarten (Kahn & Kamerman, 1987), suggesting that earlier concerns about fatigue and length of day have been minimized. We know that more time in school does not appear to be the key to improved achievement; rather, the critical determinant, as Hoegl (1985) points out, is "how that time is used" (p. 16). More time in school, however, makes possible the relaxed atmosphere of the developmentally appropriate programs that research indicates are critical to young children's achievement and well-being in school (Gornowich et al., 1974; Gullo, Bersani, Clements, & Bayless, 1986; Hatcher & Schmidt, 1980; Peck, McCaig, & Sapp, 1988). In their review of research on all-day kindergarten, researchers in the Consortium for Longitudinal Studies (1983) report that the use of developmentally appropriate instruction can have long-term positive effects on children's subsequent school performance, particularly that of low-income and non-English-speaking children. Consortium researchers noted that a longer day without an enriched curriculum had little carryover to school performance in later years.

DISCONTINUITIES BETWEEN EARLY CHILDHOOD AND ELEMENTARY PRACTICE

Early childhood educators operate from a philosophical and professional base that is not altogether congruent with those of most primary and elementary school settings (Hauser-Cram et al., 1991; Moore, 1987; Rust, 1989). The concrete, hands-on, highly individualized, and highly interactive curriculum and instructional practices of early childhood classrooms are often at odds with the abstract, paper and pencil, whole group, highly competitive atmosphere of traditional primary and elementary school classrooms (Fromberg, 1989; Moore, 1987). As Silvern (1988) writes,

> There exists a real fear that, when public schools incorporate programs for 3- and 4-year-olds, the curriculum will look more like an elementary school program than one developed to fit the needs of young children. There is also a fear that public school programs will bring a detachment between home and school that is similar to elementary schools. (p. 148)

Instructional materials and strategies, classroom management and design, scheduling staffing and custodial requirements—these are significantly different in early childhood programs from established patterns and procedures in most elementary schools (Karweit, 1988; Katz, 1991; Shepard & Smith, 1988). Achievement testing is not done in early childhood settings; it is deemed developmentally inappropriate (Kamii, 1990). Instead, evaluation is ongoing; part of the daily interaction of early childhood teachers and their students, it is designed to meet the needs of the individual child.

Developmentally appropriate practice is rare in elementary schools because few elementary teachers know and are comfortable with it; many who know about it are fearful of parental hostility and lack of administrative support if they implement instructional approaches that differ from the norm (Murawski, 1992). Then, too, early childhood teachers in elementary settings are often alone, separated from their elementary colleagues by scheduling and the content of their teaching. There are great pressures on these teachers to modify their practice so that it fits better with that of the rest of the elementary school (Rust, 1989). Inevitably, these discontinuities must be addressed and reconciled if early childhood programs are to be integrated in schools.

CHAPTER 2

Early Childhood and the
Process of Change in Schools

Since the publication of *A Nation at Risk* (National Commission on Excellence in Education, 1983), there has been growing pressure on schools to improve the performance and achievement of the nation's children, particularly the children of poverty whose ability to cope in an increasingly technological workplace is in jeopardy. To effect improvement in student achievement, it has become clear that schools themselves must change (Cohen, 1987; Graham, 1992). They must be "restructured" to allow greater flexibility in instruction, greater freedom for teachers and administrators to design and implement effective learning environments (Barth, 1990; Meier, 1992), and greater participation from parents and communities (Campbell, 1987). Early childhood education is now seen as an important tool in the effort to improve schools (Zigler, 1987). However, few who advocate early childhood programs in the schools appreciate the enormous differences in the beliefs held by early childhood educators and other professional educators about teaching, learning, school management, and the role of the school in the child's life (Campbell, 1987; Hauser-Cram et al., 1991; Moore, 1987); thus, few anticipate the difficulties of making such change take place (Elkind, 1991; Sarason, 1987). The task of articulating an early childhood philosophy and of guiding, implementing, and nurturing developmentally appropriate programs for young children in the schools must inevitably belong to early childhood educators, for there is little to suggest that the expertise for this task already exists in the schools. Examining what is known about the process of change can help.

PERSPECTIVES ON CHANGE

Change implies innovation. Innovation presumes change. The two terms are interdependent. With both, one assumes newness, a difference between what was and what is. There is a sense of movement to change and to innovation, and there is often a sense of excitement and/ or apprehension in the way individuals greet it.

The perspectives of individuals structure the ways they participate in change efforts. Perspectives on change may be strongly affected by individuals' status and affiliations and by their proximity to the change itself. Administrators, teachers, parents, and children will each perceive the introduction of an early childhood program into the schools in a different way. It is likely that district office administrators will focus most on policy issues and on costs related to staffing, transportation, space procurement, materials, and maintenance. Principals and supervisors will focus on management, staffing, schedules, and home–school relations. Teachers' concerns will relate to their students, to management, and to curriculum and instruction. Parents' perceptions of their children's welfare and progress will shape their attitude toward a new program. How young children perceive a program is gauged by their daily interactions with one another and with the program faculty as well as by their performance over time.

In his analysis of studies of educational change, House (1981) identifies three perspectives—technological, political, and cultural—that encompass the totality of viewpoints on the process of change. These perspectives, he writes, "operate implicitly" as a "'way of seeing' a problem rather than a rigid set of rules and procedures" (p. 20). From the technological perspective, change is viewed as "a relatively mechanistic process" (p. 18). So, for example, an extended morning kindergarten program, viewed from the technological perspective, would be understood as simply an hour more of school. The adjustments made by teachers, parents, and students would receive minimal, if any, attention.

"From the political perspective," writes House (1981), "innovation is a matter of conflicts and compromises among factional groups. . . . Cooperation on an innovation is viewed as problematic rather than automatic. Cooperation must result from negotiation and compromise" (p. 23). The political perspective is evident in the analysis of innovation in Kensington undertaken by Smith and Keith (1971), in Post's (1992) story of curriculum change in Joshua Gap, and in Lewis and

Miles's (1990) description of efforts to reform urban high schools. From a theoretical standpoint, the work of Weick (1982), Fullan and Steigelbauer (1991), and Deal (1990) incorporates the political perspective.

From the cultural perspective, innovation involves changing beliefs; it is a long, slow process. Conflicts and misunderstandings that arise in group situations are interpreted from the cultural perspective as conflicts in values. House (1981) writes that this perspective "harbors a more conservative, traditional view of change" (p. 35) than the other two perspectives: Change comes slowly, if at all, and can be illusory. As Elkind (1991) describes it,

> If the educational innovation is in keeping with the underlying philosophy, then it is not truly innovative and will change nothing. On the other hand, if the innovation is at variance with the underlying philosophy it will never be properly implemented and will eventually be rejected as unworkable. (p. 2)

The cultural perspective is particularly relevant to early childhood education, since, as Katz (1987) points out, "many of the contentious issues concerning young children in the schools are debated from ideological positions that are fairly resistant to change, and often accompanied by a tendency to dismiss counterevidence as deficient or inappropriate" (p. 152).

House (1981) suggests that these three perspectives "act as interpretive frameworks for understanding the change process (and) . . . may be considered as 'moral' or 'action' paradigms" (p. 19) guiding participants' responses to change. According to House, successful instances of change incorporate all three perspectives: There is a new way of doing things (technological); there has been and often continues to be negotiation (political); and there is a fundamentally different understanding of the innovation on the part of the participants (cultural).

THE PROCESS OF CHANGE

Miel (1946) wrote that "change must be social and must guarantee security and growth for those involved" (p. 23). Her sentiments are echoed often by veterans of change efforts like Mooney (1992), a principal, or May (1992), a superintendent, who guided and supported new kindergarten programs in their schools. Change is a venture off the beaten path. Not every step is known in advance; as Goffin (1992) suggests, "it does not occur in a linear or sequential fashion" (p. 104). Margin for error is to be anticipated and allowed. In early childhood innovations, May (1992) writes, "Creating time to study, to discuss, and to collectively construct the vision and develop capacities to implement developmentally appropriate practices in classrooms is a crucial support issue" (p. 56).

In the current literature on change in schools, there is growing evidence of agreement among researchers as to the nature of change. Increasingly, it is written about as a developmental, interactive process. For example, in their review of federally funded implementation efforts, Farrar, DeSanctis, and Cohen (1981) argue that the initiation and implementation of change follows a gradually evolving course and reflects the needs of a particular situation. Guiding a change effort is often uncertain and imprecise—a process of "muddling through" (Lindbloom, 1959) in which "policy is not made once and for all; it is made and remade endlessly" (p. 86). Managing change is, to quote Lindbloom, "a rough process" (p. 86). It is not a one-time event but rather a series of goal-oriented steps. These steps are often unpredictable at the outset. Studies of instances of change in schools, like those of Lewis and Miles (1990), Popkewitz (1982), Cox and Havelock (1982), Berman and McLaughlin (1978), and Smith and Keith (1971), show that successful change follows an evolutionary course that fits the needs of the setting, enjoys broad support and commitment, and involves mutual adaptation (the innovation changes and is changed by the system).

As described in the Rand Study (Berman & McLaughlin, 1978; McLaughlin & Marsh, 1978), the sequence of innovation is a three-stage process of mobilization, implementation, and institutionalization. These stages are remarkably similar to stages of change identified by Lewin (1961) as unfreezing, implementation, and refreezing. They are also similar to Clark and Guba's (1965) trial (development), installation (diffusion), and institutionalization (adoption).

Mobilization

Mobilization describes those activities surrounding the initiation of an innovation. Research by Fullan and Steigelbauer (1991) and

Berman and McLaughlin (1978) identifies the mobilization stage as the single most important stage in the change process. It includes identifying the need for change, marshaling support, and developing implementation strategies.

The mobilization process should involve what Sarason (1972) terms "confronting history": exploring individuals' relationships to the setting, "dealing with a history of structural relationships," and using "this historical knowledge for actions which maximize the chances that the new setting will be viable and in ways consistent with its values and goals" (pp. 42–43). This is the "backward look" (p. 7) that Deal (1990) describes in his discussion of school reform.

> [The first step in change is] to reach back, in research rather than nostalgic quest, to our historical roots. There we must refind and rekindle basic values, stories, ritual, or other symbols that may have been lost, forgotten, or allowed to atrophy. In the wake of our attempts to rationalize the schools, there is a rich residue of practices and wisdom that may still be valid. The second is to refocus and renegotiate the myths and values about schooling. (p. 12)

Broad-based support seems essential to the initiation of change (Bailey & Neale, 1980; Berman & McLaughlin, 1978; Burrello & Orbaugh, 1982). Lieberman and Shiman (1972) identify it as a combination of community support, district support, principal leadership, and a teacher group of "early adopters" (p. 68). Broad-based support must not be misconstrued. It means more than the enthusiasm and excitement that often accompany innovation. It means commitment. It means anticipating that there will be difficulties, and it means planning strategies for dealing with them (Sarason, 1972).

Participation in the decision-making process does not preclude effective leadership. Rather, it suggests a style of leadership that recognizes and works within the organizational and behavioral regularities of a system (Barth, 1990; Deal, 1990; Katz & Kahn, 1975; Lewis & Miles, 1990; Sarason, 1982; Weick, 1982). "Change from within," writes Morgan-Worsham (1990), "is the only way to achieve lasting improvement in an individual or a group" (p. 69).

Leadership from the district office appears to be critically important during the mobilization stage. As Hauser-Cram and colleagues (1991) describe it,

The superintendent of schools, as chief administrative officer of a
program, and the school committee, as the local policy-making
body, must understand the goals and provide unequivocal support
for a school-based program. The competition for scarce resources
is so keen and the pressures for broadening of goals so strong that
if the superintendent and the school committee are not committed
to the program, interested parents and school staff should collabo-
rate with a capable community agency that can take the lead role
in delivering early education. (p. 189)

Principals are key figures during these early stages for it is they
who can allocate time for teachers to meet and plan; it is they who
articulate the need for the innovation to the community and to the district office; it is they who create the climate of support and trust that
is necessary for an innovation to flourish. May (1992) writes, "The
advice I would offer to superintendents interested in developing appropriate practices districtwide is to implement strategies involving principals at every step" (p. 64). Innovations proposed by teachers or by
the community that do not gain support from the district office and
the principal at the outset appear to fail.

In summary, support from all levels of the school organization
during the mobilization stage of a change effort appears to be essential
to sustaining a change project. Leadership, careful planning, and commitment to the project's continuation also appear to be critical. The
underlying reasons for change and the activities that take place before
and during the mobilization stage can have a profound effect on its
implementation and on the eventual outcome of an innovation (Berman
& McLaughlin, 1978).

Implementation

Implementation describes that period during which an innovation
is tried and used in a school. During the implementation stage, the
innovation is shaped to fit the particular system using it (Berman &
McLaughlin, 1978). Implementation can be a lengthy process the outcome of which is neither guaranteed nor predictable.

Berman and McLaughlin (1978) found that school people typically
respond in one of three ways to an innovation: They may simply re-
ject it (nonimplementation); they may make it look like they are using

it, but in fact change nothing (co-optation); or they may adopt it, changing it to fit the setting and changing themselves to accommodate to it (mutual adaptation). The complexity of the innovation and the level of teacher involvement are the key indicators of which of these three responses will prevail (Fullan, Bennett, & Rolheiser-Bennett, 1990).

Whatever the focus of the change effort, its success hinges directly on teachers' willingness and ability to act on it. "If teachers are not able to join in leading such changes," writes Meier (1992), "the changes will not take place" (p. 594). Teachers should be involved in planning and decision making. Such involvement can be justified, according to Sarason (1982), on several grounds: Their involvement makes it more likely that responsibility for change will be assumed and not be attributed to others. It appears more likely that problems of attitudes and goals will surface and be dealt with. Last, and probably most important, is that such involvement increases the chance that a variety of solutions will be voiced and examined.

Innovation in education frequently necessitates helping teachers to use new technologies, new methods, or new curricula. Inservice work with teachers should be relevant (job related), practical, and ongoing (Grover, 1990). Staff development takes time and is costly. However, as Barth (1990) points out, "Probably nothing within a school has more impact on students in terms of skills development, self-confidence, or classroom behavior than the personal and professional growth of their teachers" (p. 53).

"Teachers," writes May (1992), "cannot create and sustain significant change without the active support of the administration" (p. 71). The support of the principal, in particular, is critical during the implementation phase for it is the principal who articulates the vision of the innovation and who lends credibility to the change process (Grover, 1990; May, 1992; Mooney, 1992). Principals often manage change in what Weick (1982) terms "a loosely coupled" system, that is, a system in which there is room for innovation and experimentation in individual units while others maintain their habitual practices. In a loosely coupled system, the principal works to keep the various units informed of one another's activities and to maintain a sense of commitment to the whole. Once the initial funding and enthusiasm for an innovation have gone, it is usually the principal who articulates the change to new personnel and who maintains morale.

Like the principal, a change agent is a resource and a supportive element in the change process. This person is the one who provides the practical expertise to implement the change. Change agents who appear to be most effective participate actively in the life of the school and thus are able to create a climate for mutual support and growing trust. They serve as consultants, co-workers, and models. Loucks and Cox (1982) describe them as

> individuals who "get their hands dirty" working in the school and with teachers and administrators to find out what they need, get or give training, provide assistance and support after training, and help to maintain the practice. They are the cheerleaders, building and maintaining commitment and spirit; they are the linkers, bringing new practices and skills to teachers; and they are the trouble shooters, providing help and support where needed. (p. 5)

Change agents are particularly important in early childhood innovations where there is likely to be a significant philosophical and behavioral shift required of teachers and administrators (Grover, 1990; May, 1992; Mooney, 1992; Murawski, 1992).

Community support during the implementation phase is critical (Lewis & Miles, 1990; Post, 1992). In their study of innovation, Smith and Keith (1971) provide an example of the community's importance: They found that lack of conceptual clarity between community, district office, administration, and teaching staff was one of the major reasons for Kensington's failure. Goals and values were not shared. The community was not represented in the planning of the innovation or in its implementation. In early childhood innovations, community support is essential for it is the community's concern for the next generation that gives shape and substance to the program of the schools and to the resources available for the care and education of its children.

District office support is also essential during the implementation phase not so much in terms of actual participation but rather in providing encouragement, approval, and, where necessary, material assistance.

The implementation stage, then, involves an often lengthy and uncertain process requiring high commitment and substantial participation from teachers, administrators, and community. It is the core of the change process.

Institutionalization

Lewin (1961) refers to institutionalization as "refreezing"—the period during which the innovation becomes a fixed and integral part of the day-to-day operations of the school. It is the last phase of the change process, and its outcome depends on what has happened during the change process: the way planning was done, the degree of commitment from the district (including financial commitment), and the level of involvement of participants throughout. The district office and the community, often represented by the school board, are the central actors during the institutionalization phase because it is they who set the policies that ultimately determine the fate of the innovation.

Berman and McLaughlin (1978) identify four patterns followed by school districts during the institutionalization phase.

1. *Discontinuation*—when innovations were not continued in any form
2. *Isolated continuation*—when innovations were continued by committed individuals, with minimal support or encouragement from administrators
3. *Pro forma continuation*—when the innovation or some facet of it was officially continued, but was not used extensively by teachers in their classrooms
4. *Institutionalized change*—when the innovation became part of the modus operandi at both district and classroom levels

Projects that were institutionalized bore similar characteristics: "They tended to have been successfully implemented, to have produced teacher change, and to be marked by the continued extensive use by teachers of project methods" (p. 20). Almost always, these projects could be identified at the beginning: They had district office support and administrative, teacher, and community involvement throughout.

The change process is not easy. It can be long and slow, requiring a high level of commitment and energy from those who guide it. There must be vision (May, 1992), and there must be leadership, such as that described by Sergiovanni (1990), that unites participants in pursuit of a common goal.

As the adoption of early childhood programs by schools increases, there should be growing concern about what is changing—early childhood practice or the schools—and the level of change in each. More than most change efforts, early childhood innovations impinge on deeply held beliefs about family, schooling, and the role of the community in preparing the next generation (Lazarson, 1988). Without genuine commitment to change and skilled, sustained leadership it is likely that the early childhood aspect of early childhood innovations in the schools will be lost or seriously compromised.

Part II

CASES FROM THE FIELD

CHAPTER 3

Developing the Case Studies

Case studies have the power to inform practice in ways generally available only through first-hand experience. They are used extensively in business, legal, and medical education as a means of focusing students' attention on specific issues and enabling them to explore those topics in depth. Case studies of change efforts in schools function in much the same way for administrators, policy-makers, and change agents, enabling them to learn about the practical details of innovation that are often missing, as Maguire (1971) points out, from theoretical research on change. The theoretical research on change, according to Goldenberg and Gallimore (1991),

> does not provide knowledge about local sites, the contexts in which reforms either succeed or fail. . . . If schools are small local cultures then researchers and reformers need to know more about the cultural context of the objects of their reform efforts. This includes, for example, understanding the local schemas or beliefs that shape perceptions and drive behaviors in "unselfconscious" (Geertz, 1984, p. 125) ways. (p. 12)

Case studies have the power to make this "local knowledge" about schools available to support change agents, administrators, and policy-makers in their work of shaping and guiding innovations.

While there are numerous studies of all-day kindergarten, four-year-old, and other preschool programs in schools, there are few, if any, in-depth case studies that focus specifically on the process of implementing these and other early childhood innovations in schools. Thus, there is little in the way of practical knowledge to guide the work of advocates for early childhood education in the schools or of practitioners and policy-makers attempting to bring early childhood programs into schools. The case studies that follow this chapter are intended to fill that void. Both are composites of studies that I have conducted. While neither describes a particular school system, both are faithful to the experiences I have had as a researcher and consultant in a variety of school districts engaged in implementing all-day kindergarten programs. I have intentionally chosen different roles in each of them to provide the reader with as much detail as possible on the various perspectives and issues that are likely to be encountered by those attempting to bring early childhood programs into the schools.

METHOD

In order to develop these case studies, I used field research methods. Schwartz and Schwartz (1955) describe field research as a process of "registering" (which is simultaneous with the event), "interpreting" (giving it significance), and "recording." The focus of the research is social process or social organization, which, even if it involves only two people, can be infinitely complex. The field researcher presumes that the actual definition of the setting resides in the setting itself. The goal of the research is analytic description that accurately and faithfully represents the contextual framework of the participants. In field research, Ianni (1977) writes, "the emphasis is on allowing the design of the research to remain somewhat flexible and subject to change throughout the work" (p. 12).

Strauss (1980) emphasizes the temporal, developmental character of field research. Because the research is conducted over a period of time, the field researcher can be involved in two stages of investigation simultaneously as one proposition is being refined while others may just be coming to the surface of awareness. Furthermore, as the situation under investigation becomes more familiar, the researcher begins to make choices about what data to gather and how to gather them. Thus, field research is a process of continual evaluation, which is both simultaneous and retrospective.

The task of the field researcher is to observe, record, describe, and synthesize. Generally, the researcher follows a multi-step process. As described by Festinger and Katz (1953) and Strauss and colleagues (1964), these steps include planning and data gathering, making "sense of the massive flow of events" (Strauss et al., 1969, p. 25), formulating a research design, and analyzing. In these final stages, the researcher is testing hypotheses, looking critically at the data, "searching," as Strauss and colleagues point out, for "negative, or qualifying, as well as for supporting instances" (p. 25).

In developing the studies of Rosedale and Middle City, I took on the role of a participant observer and used the tools of field research: observation, interviewing, questionnaires, document analysis, and "participation with self-analysis" (McCall & Simon, 1969, p. 3). In Rosedale, I was an administrative intern in the elementary school. As a former teacher/director in a private school in the district, I had an indepth knowledge of the setting that is not usually available to researchers. In Middle City, I was a consultant first to the school district and later to an individual school. This is a more customary role for a researcher and participant observer.

In both settings, I relied on my field notes—daily logs of my work—as well as conversations and interviews with various participants; review of documents such as articles, newsletters, memos, and letters that were relevant to the all-day kindergarten programs and to understanding the districts; and questionnaires that were developed in each of the districts sampling community support for all-day kindergarten.

FIELD RESEARCH

Because the experiences and values that a researcher brings to a study shape the method and focus of observation and can act to distort the lens through which data are viewed, it is essential that some biographical material be included in order to help the reader evaluate the perspective taken in these case studies.

The Researcher

I have been involved in education for almost 25 years as an early childhood educator and a teacher educator. Drawing on training I received in the Montessori method, my reading about the British Infant Schools, and work on open classrooms that had been part of my master's program, I started and taught in a preschool version of the one-room schoolhouse—a multi-age preschool/kindergarten for three- to six-year-old children in Rosedale, the site of the case study on which Chapter 4 is based. Later, I helped to start a second such program; I directed and taught there for seven years.

In addition to my work in these schools, I have taught kindergarten in the public schools and math and science as a volunteer with second- through sixth-grade children in Rosedale. I have also served on the board of trustees of an early childhood school. I have been involved in teacher education as a cooperating teacher for local college programs and as a teacher educator with the American Montessori Society and in several university programs.

During the year of my study, I served as assistant to the principal of Rosedale Elementary School. This enabled me to complete the requirements for an administrative internship as well as collect the data for my study, and it involved me in many facets of school life.

Having directed and taught in a preschool in Rosedale, I was familiar with the personalities, roles, and histories of many in the community as well as with the recent history of the school district. I had taught many of the children in the school system and interacted with their families as well as with public school personnel. This familiarity could be considered both a strength and a liability. My personal knowledge and experience as teacher, administrator, and colleague may have given me a unique sensitivity to the perspectives of each of the participants. At the same time, my extensive history in the Rosedale community required that I exercise caution regarding, first, the weight of my own prior opinions in shaping my interpretation of events during the year of my study and, second, the effects of participants' prior knowledge of me on the information they revealed to me and how they interacted with me.

In Middle City, I did not have the same closeness to the school system. I was a consultant, one of many that the district hired over the year. Because of my reputation as an early childhood educator and researcher in the area of all-day kindergarten, I was hired to work directly with the associate superintendent and the Kindergarten Task Force to assess the viability of all-day kindergarten in the district and to develop a plan for its implementation. My knowledge of the school system came from reading about it, analyzing materials that the school system provided, and interactions with the associate superintendent, members of the Kindergarten Task Force, and my colleague, Dr. Burton Baxter, who had worked with the school district to implement a number of earlier innovations.

Entering the Field

The way in which a researcher enters the field and is perceived in the setting is critical to the conduct of field research. Entering the field is important, according to Johnson (1975), because

> The conditions under which an initial entree is negotiated may have important consequences for how the research is socially defined by the members of the setting. These social definitions will have a bearing on the extent to which the members trust a social researcher, and the existence of relations of trust between an observer and the members of a setting is essential to the production of an objective report, one which retains the integrity of the actor's perspective and its social context. (pp. 50–51)

As I spent time in these settings, I was keenly aware of the ways in which my roles as early childhood teacher, university professor, researcher, consultant (in Middle City), and administrative intern (in Rosedale) shaped both my interactions with the participants and their perceptions of me. I found that the closer individuals were to being the focus of my research, the more specific were their questions about my work. From the principals, there was general desire that my extensive experience in early childhood be made available to the kindergarten teachers. The teachers were concerned about the level of my involvement in the determination of curriculum and in classroom management.

Participant Observation

Participant observation is described by Kluckhohn (1940) as "conscious and systematic sharing, in so far as circumstances permit, in the life activities and, on occasion, in the interests and affects of a group of persons" (p. 331). Schwartz and Schwartz (1955) describe the roles of the participant observer as passive and active. In the passive role, the participant observer "assumes that the more passive he is, the less he will affect the situation and the greater will be his opportunity to observe events as they develop" (p. 348). The researcher is likely to be detached from the situation, and therefore unlikely to overidentify with the participants, but may be resented for this detachment by those observed, as in the case of Wolcott's (1977) experience with the Planning, Programming and Budgeting System (PPBS) innovation and mine with the Ad Hoc Committee in Rosedale (Rust, 1984). I suspect this resentment has to do with lack of trust and not being perceived as useful to participants.

In the active role, the participant observer, according to Schwartz and Schwartz (1955), "maximizes his participation with the observed in order to gather data and attempts to integrate his role with other roles in the social structure. . . . His intuition is to experience the life of the observed so that he can better observe and understand it" (p. 349).

The active role may give a participant observer more insight into the meanings of a situation, but it can lead to too strong an affective identification with the participants—the situation of "going native" in which the researcher can become so close to the situation as to lose objectivity. The active role can work as Rauh's (1978) description of the helping teacher or Loucks and Cox's (1982) description of change agents suggests.

Kluckhohn (1940) draws a distinction between general and specific roles of the participant observer. He describes the general role as "that role which one plays without reference to any particular person. It is played in relation to various persons, and, although it becomes a part of the specific relationship with each of these persons, it is general in terms of all of them" (p. 332). The basic factors affecting general roles are "objective states such as sex, age, position in a caste or class, or race" (p. 333). A specific role is that which one plays in relation to a definite person, for example, a spouse, parent, or teacher.

Because the goal of this research was the development of a clearer understanding of the process of change and of how participants in that process communicate about it with one another, I chose a specific, active participant observer role so that I could maintain a high level of contact with participants in both settings. Throughout the school year in Rosedale, I assumed various roles in the school: colleague, teacher, administrative intern, and committee member. Because my particular focus was the kindergarten, much of my time was spent there or with work that was related to the program. Over time, it became clear that I had gained the teachers' trust through my work with them and the children. To them, I was a peer; to the kindergarten children, I was a teacher. In the role of administrative intern, I experienced more difficulty. While the label facilitated entry to the kindergarten classrooms and frequent contact with other teachers, administrators, and parents without giving me the responsibility to the program that the roles of consultant or change agent might imply, I found that some of the elementary school teachers perceived me as "the ears" of the administration. These teachers were not as open with me as they were with their peers. Parents, too, were somewhat inhibited. The job classification "administrative intern" was unfamiliar to them; it did not carry any clear role expectation. On occasion, it was clear that the fact that I was well known in Rosedale was an inhibiting factor in my interactions with administrators other than the principal. To those on the Ad Hoc Committee who were new to Rosedale, I was an "outsider"—one who according to Kluckhohn (1940) and Vidich (1969) is never completely assimilated by the group. Because the superintendent specifically proscribed my participating in or in any way attempting to influence the work of the Ad Hoc Committee, at the committee's meetings I could only act as an observer—the passive role that Schwartz and Schwartz (1955) describe. It was not until I interviewed each member after their report was complete that the new people, in particular, got to know me.

In Middle City, my relationship with the Kindergarten Task Force was quite different. I was one of two consultants responsible for guiding and directing the group's endeavor. My credibility with the members of the Task Force was predicated on my following through on promises made and providing the resources essential to our work. In the few months of work with the Middle City kindergarten teachers and school principal during the year following the Task Force meetings, I was able to develop close ties similar to my relationships with the teachers and principal in Rosedale.

IDENTIFICATION OF PARTICIPANTS

Drawing on my conception of change as a social process, I structured my analysis of these all-day kindergarten initiatives by focusing on relationships among participants using the technique of "network analysis" described by Ianni (1977). Network analysis involves discerning interpersonal links between participants, delimiting the social group, and determining power relationships within the group. The network concept enabled me to discern how information on and understandings of the innovations were communicated among participants. It also helped me to identify the key actors or the leaders in both settings. This was particularly important in Rosedale, where the complexity of interactions over the year of study made it imperative that I understand the dynamics of the setting.

Generally, I applied the rubric used by Smith and Keith (1971) in *Anatomy of Educational Innovation* according to which participants' status is determined by their proximity to the innovation and their involvement in shaping it. More specifically, persons were identified as participants in the change process by official and unofficial consensus. Those whom the official documents of the school system named as participants were the official participants. Those whom two or more of these persons identified as integral to the process were the unofficial participants. These included parents, the children, teachers on other grade levels, and the community—and me, the researcher.

This latter process of participant/participant designation is like Zelditch's (1962) technique of sequential sampling for testing the reliability of informant information: Information provided by one informant is compared with information from a second, third, and fourth. If a similar story emerges from these several sources, then the researcher may begin to believe in the reliability of the information. If not, the researcher must look further. Zelditch (1962) writes, "The pitfall here is that we may be deceived by a homogeneous 'pocket' within which all members agree but which does not necessarily represent all structural parts of S. For this reason, we try to use representative informants, each from different status groups" (p. 573).

The identification of "unofficial" participants in Rosedale and Middle City followed a similar strategy. Using the technique of network analysis (Ianni, 1972) described above to secure information from a broad cross-section of the communities and comparing stories from official participants, the unofficial participants were identified.

DATA COLLECTION AND ANALYSIS

In attempting to organize and structure the data gathered from observations, interviews, and analyses of documents, I made use of several analytical methods derived from study of the work of other field researchers. Among the most useful of these was the technique of event analysis used by Smith and Keith (1971) in their study of the Kensington innovation. They followed the development of the organization through three main periods of time looking carefully at the types and levels of involvement of all the participants as they pertained to the key events of each of those periods. In developing these case studies, I was able to organize the data from my research around several key events and to analyze the participants' activities as they related to those events.

Another strategy that proved useful was the method of theoretical sampling described by Strauss (1980). It is a process of data collection

> whereby the analyst simultaneously collects, codes, and analyzes his data and decides what data to collect next and where to find them in order to develop his theory as it emerges. This process of data collection is controlled by the emergent theory. As is usual in field work, initial decisions for data collection are based only on a general initial framework, not on a preconceived theoretical framework. The basic question in theoretical sampling is: What groups or subgroups does one turn to next in data collection? And for what theoretical purpose? In short, how should one select multiple comparison groups? Since the possibilities of multiple comparisons are infinite, groups must be chosen according to theoretical criteria. (p. 197)

It is clear that my observations were guided by my general conception of innovation as a social process embedded in the larger social framework of schools. Operating from this theoretical stance, I identified and limited the universe of data to those key events, participants, observational settings, and documents that were directly related to the kindergarten innovations in these settings.

LIMITATIONS, RELIABILITY, AND VALIDITY

The potential limitations of the field research method are observer bias; lack of quantitative, measurable data; and too strong an identification with the participants or too great an involvement in the process being observed, both of which can lead to a narrow focus and limited data base. However, a "thick description" (Geertz, 1973) like this one of specific change efforts can provide researchers, change agents, policymakers, and administrators with practical knowledge of the change process. It is not intended to be definitive of research on change or on the conduct of early childhood programs in the elementary school. Rather, it is intended as complementary to other studies of change as a means of enhancing our knowledge of the change process. As Goldenberg and Gallimore (1991) point out,

> It is very likely the prospect of reforming schools depends on a better understanding of the interplay between research knowledge and local knowledge. The more we know about the dynamics of this interplay, the more likely it is that research can have an effect on the nature and effectiveness of schools. (p. 2)

The reliability of the data can be estimated in a number of ways, including a process of cross-checking, seeking supporting and non-supporting instances that can help to establish the credibility of a researcher's observations. The use of multiple observation methods is also helpful in establishing reliability and can serve to enhance the cross-checking process. The use of the techniques of participant observation, informant interviewing, and document analysis in these case studies provided access to many perspectives on the innovation process both in Rosedale and in Middle City; they were useful in determining the evolution of the change process in these settings.

INTRODUCTION TO THE CASE STUDIES

In the following chapters, I present two case studies of all-day kindergarten initiatives. Both are composites of initiatives in which I was involved. The first, "Kindergarten Change in Rosedale," is based on the study I completed for my dissertation (Rust, 1984). Here, I have taken the perspective of an "insider," one who knows the system, the participants, the way things work. I chose this perspective because it is the one most often available to teachers and administrators managing early childhood programs in their schools. It shows how complex and "messy" change is, and, for that reason alone, it should be valuable to change agents and policy-makers who are not usually enmeshed in the daily life of schools and classrooms. But for those teachers, administrators, parents, and others whose day-to-day work with children and their families is the shape and substance of schools, the

Rosedale story may be particularly valuable, for it holds important lessons about working for change within the system.

The second case study, "Kindergarten Planning in Middle City," is based on my work as a consultant to school systems developing all-day kindergarten programs. Here, I have chosen the perspective of an "outsider," one who is not involved in the day-to-day work of the school and who is not well known to the participants. This is the more customary role for change agents initiating and guiding early childhood programs in schools. This case study focuses on a successful planning process, and, as such, should be informative to the work of change agents, whether insiders or outsiders.

I have written these cases in the first person to bring you, the reader, closer to my perspective as a participant observer, thereby engaging you in the action and providing a first-hand understanding of the complex issues that surround efforts to bring early childhood practice into schools.

CHAPTER 4

Kindergarten Change in Rosedale

This chapter focuses on two simultaneous innovation efforts in a small suburban school district: One is the attempt to initiate all-day kindergarten; the other is the implementation of an extended morning kindergarten. The chapter is designed to give the reader a sense of the complexity of the change process and its impact on the daily life of a school system in a community that I have called Rosedale.

Rosedale is an affluent, largely white-collar suburb of a large city. The school district is small, 1,200 students, with one high school, one middle school, and one elementary school. It is small enough to engender a feeling of community and large enough to be able to offer a comprehensive college preparatory program for the majority of its students.

While Rosedale is largely residential, few buy their first houses here; instead, families with school-age children move here drawn by the excellent reputation of the schools. Rosedale parents play an active role in their children's education. Parent volunteers are in the schools daily. The school board elections and the budget vote each June are a major local political event.

At the time of this study, the Rosedale schools were experiencing a decline in enrollments that was particularly acute in the elementary school where, during each of the previous five years, at least one elementary teacher had been laid off or offered a part-time position in the kindergarten and the one full-time kindergarten teacher, as least senior faculty member, was in danger of losing her job. During the previous spring, the elementary school principal had proposed all-day kindergarten for the district in an effort to prevent the loss of the full-time kindergarten teacher. In doing so, she inadvertently ignited a controversy within the community and within the school district administration that resulted in the school board's deciding to approve the implementation of an extended morning kindergarten program for the fall and to appoint an ad hoc committee to study the issue of all-day kindergarten.

KEY PARTICIPANTS

The Principal—Mrs. Barbara Thornton

At the time this story begins, Barbara Thornton had been principal of Rosedale Elementary School for seven years. Few elementary school parents could remember a time when Barbara Thornton had not been the principal. However, she had been a classroom teacher at Rosedale for 12 years before that and had worked with all but two of the current faculty during those years. The teachers liked her. They came to her for advice. They invited her into their classrooms. Among them, she had a reputation for being able to handle difficult issues regarding staff professionally and with sensitivity and decisiveness.

Both physically and in its ambiance, the 30-year-old elementary school reflected Barbara Thornton's philosophy of education and her attitude toward teaching and leadership. Classroom doors were generally open to the hallways so that there was always the sound of children in the building. Mrs. Thornton knew many of the children by name. She seemed to have her finger on the pulse of the school.

In her years as principal, Barbara Thornton had introduced a number of innovations that had become part of the working operation of the school and part of the school's identity. One of the most successful was a Pupil Study Team (which functioned as the now state-mandated Committee on the Handicapped) and a program for the gifted and talented. She saw herself as having always been in the vanguard of educational change and as having been somewhat unorthodox in her methods. As an example, she described for me the way she went about developing the program for the gifted and talented.

I was deeply interested in it. Several parents were concerned about their children and wanted the school to address their needs. There was a teacher on the staff who was also deeply interested in the subject. Together, we proposed and held an assembly that the children ran. It was extraordinary; those parents and school board members who

were in the audience were astounded by the quality and
depth of the children's production.

Launching an innovation, particularly in gifted education, in this way is really frowned upon because the children are put in the limelight and made to appear different.
The program never would have taken off without the initial
federal seed money. I spent the next several years working
with parents and teachers laying the groundwork to insure
the continuation of the program once that funding dried up.

With this innovation, as with others, she involved parents and
teachers in developing the design of the program and in its implementation. She continued forcefully to articulate the need to maintain and
improve it long after the initial enthusiasm for it had waned and even
in the face of indifference and sometimes hostility from the community and lack of genuine support from the superintendent and the school
board. It was strong and viable within the context of the elementary
school and received support from teachers on each grade level.

The Full-Time Kindergarten Teacher—Mrs. Doris Cohen

When she became the principal of Rosedale Elementary School,
Barbara Thornton hired Doris Cohen to teach in the kindergarten. Mrs.
Cohen came to Rosedale with 13 years of early childhood and kindergarten teaching experience and five years of administrative work as the
director of a large private preschool program.

Barbara Thornton and Doris Cohen worked well together. Mrs.
Thornton had come to rely on Mrs. Cohen's opinions concerning kindergarten and early childhood education. Parents shared the principal's
viewpoint. To many in the community, Doris Cohen was synonymous
with the kindergarten. As declining enrollments forced staff cutbacks
and fewer classes on the kindergarten level, she appeared to be the
stabilizing force in a sea of change: During this time, she was the only
full-time kindergarten teacher, was solely responsible for the development and coordination of the kindergarten curriculum, and trained those
full-time, upper-grade teachers who were reassigned to teach part-time
in the kindergarten. For Doris Cohen, the stress of teaching her own
classes and planning and training teachers for the others was great, but

she did it, she said, "out of loyalty to the elementary school, the children, the principal, and the district."

Mrs. Cohen felt that much of her work in Rosedale had involved bringing an early childhood/developmental approach to teaching in the kindergarten. During her years there, she was continually involved in articulating her perspective on young children and their education through teacher training and through redesign of the kindergarten curriculum. Doris Cohen had been reading about and discussing all-day kindergarten for at least six years before she was able to convince Barbara Thornton that it was a good idea for Rosedale. Once she had Mrs. Thornton's support, the effort to bring all-day kindergarten to Rosedale began. Mrs. Cohen got it started; Mrs. Thornton was its guide.

The Superintendent—Dr. Ted Blake

In his seven years as superintendent in Rosedale, Ted Blake steered a course for the district that took it from its vanguard position in the 1960s "open classroom" movement to a middle of the road, even slightly conservative stance. Dr. Blake came to Rosedale the same year that Barbara Thornton became the principal of the elementary school. He found a school district deeply divided over educational and financial issues. His predecessor, a strong-minded and articulate spokesman for the innovations of the 1960s, had, with the combined force of his own personality and an energetic school board, pushed through major changes in the district that drastically altered its educational character. Two factors in the early 1970s—an ambitious building program and increasing teacher militancy regarding wages, benefits, and working conditions—had led to financial strain in the district.

Ted Blake arrived at the moment when the pendulum seemed to have begun to swing back from a point far left of center. A new school board was in place. This board represented old-time Rosedale. Its members had been living in Rosedale during the innovations of the late 1960s and felt that these had significantly tarnished the educational reputation of the district.

Dr. Blake was new to the area and new to the superintendency. Without a history in the community to brand him as either liberal or conservative, he was able to initiate conversations and to negotiate understandings between parties who had previously been unable or unwilling to speak together. His leadership was characterized by his ability to bridge the gaps between liberals and conservatives and between old and new Rosedale residents.

The community found Dr. Blake accessible and attentive. Among the teachers, he was considered a capable and fair administrator. Many expressed personal warmth toward him and enjoyed contact with him. Dr. Blake worked well and closely with the principals and other school administrators within the district.

Dr. Blake's leadership in the district could be described as more political than educational. During his tenure, new programs in the district were generally initiated by teachers and by principals—not in the superintendent's office. In general, his support of an innovation reflected board approval. There were instances of Dr. Blake's standing behind an innovation despite lack of approval from the board, as he did for Barbara Thornton's program for the gifted and talented, but these were rare.

When Barbara Thornton proposed the concept of an all-day kindergarten to Dr. Blake, she met with a noncommittal response and was charged with gathering more information on the subject. As the proposal developed and was discussed between them, it became clear that Dr. Blake would not support it.

The School Board

The Rosedale School Board is made up of five individuals who are elected to office by vote of the community in an annual election. Their terms of office range from one to three years depending on the plurality of votes each receives. All of the individuals who served on the board during the period of this study had been residents of Rosedale for at least 12 years. Three had served two or more consecutive terms on the board. Two were newly elected to the board but had considerable experience with the schools as PTA officers and "in school" volunteers. None of the school board members had made their career in education. The three male members of the board were business executives; both women were housewives. While all but one member of the school board had children in the Rosedale schools, only one member, a male, had a child young enough to be in the elementary school. None had kindergarten- or preschool-age children.

Longtime residents were more likely than young parents to know the members of the school board personally since they were more likely to have children in middle and upper grades. For the younger families in town, the primary opportunities for personal interaction with school board members were coffees held for candidates in private homes prior to school board elections. Less personal lines of communication were the monthly school board meetings and the district newsletter.

This school board had developed a reputation in the community for fiscal responsibility and for having taken a firm stand in favor of quality education. They took credit for a rise in college board scores, an increase in the number of new families attracted to the town because of its schools, and changing the image of the schools from the open classroom situation of the late 1960s and early 1970s to a stable and academically excellent environment.

Regarding the issue of all-day kindergarten, the board, like the parents, appeared largely uninformed. Other than the arguments that they had heard between the superintendent and the principal and outside of my review of the research on all-day kindergarten (which the principal had provided them) (Rust, 1982), they had little education on the issue. Like the parents whom they represented, their focus was on the appropriateness of an all-day/every day kindergarten program for young children.

The Part-Time Kindergarten Teachers

Mrs. Ruth Fletcher. Ruth Fletcher began teaching in Rosedale when the concept of the open classroom was in vogue. During her eight years in the district she taught on a number of grade levels, most recently fifth grade. When declining enrollments forced a redesign of the grade structure in Rosedale, Mrs. Fletcher was given the choice of being excessed or of accepting a part-time position in the kindergarten. She chose a half-time kindergarten position. She worked closely with Mrs. Cohen during the early part of that year as she became acclimated to working with young children and learning the kindergarten curriculum. That January, she accepted an afternoon kindergarten position in neighboring Rockwood. In reminiscing with me about that first year of kindergarten teaching, Mrs. Fletcher was still a little amazed by all that she had done and by how much she had learned from the two very different settings.

Mrs. Fletcher approached teaching as a profession at which she

considered herself very competent. She brought to her teaching interests in science, mathematics, and computers. During her teacher training and in college, she developed a keen interest in developmental
psychology. She had prepared to be an early childhood teacher. She
had strong organizational skills that were evidenced not only in her
ability to juggle the two kindergarten programs but also in her union
involvement and coordination of a conference session for the entire
district during National Education Week.

As she talked about teaching with me, Ruth Fletcher described
opportunities to talk with children and to explore ideas as being her
favorite part of the process. She tried, she said, to incorporate times
for that kind of verbal exchange in the schedule of her fifth grade. She
was pleased to find that kindergartners, like fifth graders, seemed to
enjoy those times, too.

Mrs. Fletcher had a good working relationship with the principal.
She did not provide the principal with the philosophical and pedagogical
support that Mrs. Cohen was able to give, but she did follow Barbara
Thornton's lead and worked willingly within the guidelines established
by her. Mrs. Fletcher also worked well with the superintendent, with
whom she planned the conference during National Education Week and
with whom she frequently met regarding union business.

Mrs. Fletcher supported the idea of a longer kindergarten day.
Along with Mrs. Cohen, she developed the curriculum for the Extended
Morning Kindergarten Program. She brought to this planning process
a perceptual/motor training curriculum that she had used during the
previous year in Rockwood. Throughout the year, she made herself
available for extensive planning after the morning kindergarten session—time that often went far beyond that for which she was contracted.

Mrs. Donna Weaver. Donna Weaver was the youngest and least
experienced of the three kindergarten teachers. She was hired by the
superintendent one day before school officially opened. She had been
one of two final candidates for the part-time (.6) position out of a field
of close to 30. She had graduated from college with a degree in psychology and with elementary school teacher certification. Her first few
years of teaching were in public schools. Immediately prior to teaching in Rosedale, she had worked as a head teacher in a Montessori
school. She had sought a public school position in order to obtain health
benefits and a better salary.

Mrs. Weaver quickly espoused the goals of the new kindergarten program and joined in the "team" effort to make it work. She accepted the classroom prepared for her by Mrs. Cohen and worked within the parameters of the curriculum that had already been designed.

Both Mrs. Cohen and Mrs. Fletcher responded positively to Mrs. Weaver. At first, the efforts of both went to guiding Mrs. Weaver through the labyrinth of new material and the new school setting. Mrs. Cohen took time at the end of each day to work with Mrs. Weaver, answering her questions and explaining details of the next day's session. Within weeks, Mrs. Weaver had mastered the schedule and routines of the Rosedale kindergarten. She began to contribute to the group's planning and to make her opinions known. She became a full and valued member of the team of kindergarten teachers.

Early in November, Donna Weaver shared with me her positive assessment of the Rosedale school district. She was particularly impressed with Barbara Thornton. She was positive about the team of teachers with whom she was working and about the evolution of the Extended Morning Program. Her only concern about the program at that point was its potential impact on the curriculum of the first grade. She felt that the two curricula should be kept separate: The curriculum of the first grade should be primarily geared (as it then was) to the teaching of reading. She felt that the kindergarten program should meet the needs and specifications of the Rosedale community and that the community should have a major voice in determining the outcome of the kindergarten innovation.

BACKGROUND

In the year before I began my work in Rosedale, Barbara Thornton began planning for all-day kindergarten by enlisting the help of the Community Liaison Committee, a subcommittee of the elementary school PTA. Together, they designed a questionnaire to ascertain community opinion on all-day kindergarten. Barbara Thornton believed that a call-back program or an alternate day program would never be considered by the superintendent or the school board; thus, the questionnaire that she and the committee developed focused exclusively on all-day kindergarten. The questionnaire was sent in January *only* to families of then current kindergartners and families of children who would enter kindergarten the following autumn or thereafter—those who, the committee and principal decided, would be directly affected by an all-day kindergarten program. The questionnaire was one of the few avenues other than conversations with parents and with the Community Liaison Committee that Barbara Thornton used to sample community sentiment on the issue of all-day kindergarten. She did not, for example, hold parent coffees or write an open letter to the community.

Sampling Parents' Opinions

In all, 200 questionnaires were sent out to parents of young children; 163 were returned.

- 77% had two or more children.
- 74% had direct experience with kindergarten either currently or in the past.
- 33% had children who would be in the next year's kindergarten class.
- 46% had children entering kindergarten later than the following year.
- 88% had children in preschool. Only one respondent had not sent her older children to preschool and was not planning on preschool for her younger children.

These parents expressed strong approval for all-day kindergarten: 69% felt their child would benefit from an all-day program. Approval was highest among parents whose children had kindergarten and/or preschool experience.

Although comments were not requested, parents wrote all over the questionnaires, expressing concerns and posing questions that fell into several broad categories: curriculum, schedule and readiness, advantages and disadvantages, impetus behind the proposal, cost, and staffing.

The questionnaire was interpreted by many in the community as the announcement of firm plans to institute all-day kindergarten. It was not perceived as the fact-finding document that its designers had intended it to be. It seemed that within hours of its release, parents and others in the community mobilized to protest. The principal, school board members, and the superintendent received dozens of phone calls;

small groups of parents met to discuss the questionnaire and the issue of all-day kindergarten. Parents who felt comfortable talking with teachers shared their sentiments with them.

On an evening early in March, Barbara Thornton convened an open meeting at Rosedale Elementary School on the subject of all-day kindergarten. She had gathered together a panel of early childhood experts to discuss the implications of an all-day program. After the panel presentation, Barbara Thornton and Doris Cohen presented the results of the questionnaire and research on all-day kindergarten. They ended their presentation with a suggested full-day schedule.

When I talked with people who had been in the audience that night, it seemed evident to me that feelings ran deep on this topic in the community. Many went to the meeting convinced that all-day kindergarten was going to be a certainty in Rosedale and that it had been engineered behind their backs. As in the responses to the questionnaire, concern about length of the school day and early academic pressure figured in much of the discussion. One member of the audience, a psychologist, was reported to have attributed the high incidence of teenage suicide in a neighboring town to early academic pressure in the kindergarten and warned of a similar fate for Rosedale if the all-day concept was implemented. Division among working and nonworking mothers was also evident in this meeting: Their debate centered on child care (some equated all-day kindergarten with child care) and on the question of whether the community should support a program for parents who did not choose to stay home to raise their children.

Another community meeting on the subject was held later in March. This time it was hosted by the Rosedale School Board on a Saturday morning at the elementary school. The discussion was heated. Members of the audience questioned the reasons behind the all-day initiative. Divisions within the parents' ranks and between the parents and the school were once again evident. The principal presented several options for the future organization of the kindergarten and reiterated her conviction, based on her study of the research, that all-day/ every day kindergarten was the optimal program for Rosedale. At this point, no action was taken by the school board. The community was left with promise of continued discussion between the administration and the board aimed at resolving some of the issues raised in these two meetings.

Response

In the aftermath of the March meetings, the parents and the professionals went in different directions. Barbara Thornton continued to campaign for an all-day program. In letters to and in personal conversations with the superintendent, she articulated her viewpoint that it was the best and most reasonable solution to the problem of lengthening the kindergarten day. The superintendent strongly disagreed. They argued about it in closed sessions before the school board. Their disagreement made the members of the school board very uncomfortable.

Many in the larger Rosedale community declined further involvement in the kindergarten issue. In informal discussions with me, some members of this "silent majority" claimed ignorance of the issue; some told me that they feared the new program would add to their tax burden; some, who were parents of older children and had no preschoolers, felt that it would have benefited their children; they were, however, reluctant to press their viewpoint on a new group of parents.

A small group of parents of primary-age children (eight years and younger) informally gathered to study the issue and to bring pressure on the administration of the Rosedale school district to "reconsider" and to involve the community in the decision-making process. Through talk and petitions circulated throughout the community, this small parent-pressure group felt that it had succeeded in moving the school board and the superintendent to a reconsideration of the kindergarten plan and to the formation of an ad hoc committee to study the kindergarten. Six of the eight members of this group later joined the Ad Hoc Committee.

In April, the school board directed Dr. Blake to propose an alternative to the principal's all-day kindergarten proposal. The superintendent recommended an extended morning kindergarten program—an hour more of kindergarten each day. This plan was approved and adopted by the school board in May. It was implemented the following September. In July, the board announced its intent to form an ad hoc committee to study the kindergarten and possible alternatives to it, and to make recommendations to them, and it issued an invitation to members of the community to join the committee. The board did not publicly comment on the kindergarten issue again until the Ad Hoc Committee report was submitted the following March.

The Ad Hoc Committee

By September, 17 people had volunteered for the Ad Hoc Committee—15 women, two men. All were accepted by the school board and the superintendent. I was invited by the superintendent to join the committee as an observer. The school board appointed one of its female members as liaison between the committee and the board.

There were no official representatives from the Rosedale elementary school faculty. I was later told by one of the Rosedale teachers and by the teachers union president that the union had been offered the option of placing a member on the committee and chose not to exercise the option for fear of misrepresenting the work of the kindergarten teacher and the principal. When I asked them about it, the chairperson of the Ad Hoc Committee and the kindergarten teacher, Mrs. Cohen, claimed ignorance of this option.

There was no liaison established between the Ad Hoc Committee and the school personnel, and in many ways they were isolated from one another during their respective studies of the kindergarten program. The superintendent had expressly counseled me not to participate in the committee's activities; I was to be a neutral observer. Thus, when the committee wanted information about a program in the elementary school, a committee member had to call the principal and make arrangements for a conference with her or with the appropriate teacher. By the same token, the principal and teachers had no formal access to the work of the committee unless they contacted the committee chairperson or a committee member. Although I generally "debriefed" with the principal during the morning following an Ad Hoc Committee meeting, I did not discuss the committee meetings with the kindergarten teachers.

The 17 members of the committee were all parents of children in Rosedale Elementary School. Fourteen were also parents of preschoolers and thus anticipated using the Rosedale kindergarten in the future. Only four had never had children enrolled in the kindergarten. Seven were parents of children in the new Extended Morning Program.

All the members were college graduates. Three had experience as teachers: One was working as an elementary school teacher; one had previously taught second grade; one had previously taught in and directed early childhood centers. Eight were involved in careers: the elementary school teacher, a psychiatrist, a social worker, three in business, and two who were pursuing advanced degrees in social work. Nine were involved in child rearing; they did not describe this as a career. Three of the latter reported having careers prior to child rearing.

All but two of the committee members (both new to Rosedale) knew at least one other member of the Ad Hoc Committee. Six of the members had worked together in the informal group of parents, described earlier, that had formed the previous spring subsequent to the January questionnaire and the March meetings to bring pressure on the district to study the kindergarten issue further. They felt that their pressure had led to the formation of the Ad Hoc Committee. This group worked together and voted almost as a block throughout their tenure on the Ad Hoc Committee.

Three members of the committee were well known to each other by virtue of having lived in Rosedale for more than 10 years. Among these was the chairperson. She, like the two other longtime residents, had done extensive committee work in the community. Six other members of the committee also had extensive committee experience—all but one within the Rosedale community. Two of the long-term residents claimed a great deal of knowledge about the local schools. They and the former nursery school director became valuable sources of information to other members of the committee about children and education.

BEGINNINGS

With the opening of school, the emotion of the previous spring regarding the kindergarten program seemed to have subsided. Parents were willingly sending their children to kindergarten and appeared to be accommodating to the new extended morning schedule; through the appointment of the Ad Hoc Committee they had gained a voice in decisions about the kindergarten program. In the elementary school, there were now three kindergarten teachers instead of two. Doris Cohen was the only full-time teacher. Ruth Fletcher, previously teaching half-time, was hired at .6 time, and Donna Weaver, the new kindergarten teacher, was also to be hired at .6 time. The principal and kindergarten teachers were prepared to implement the new program; they had begun to develop a plan for its evaluation.

Dr. Blake remained firm in his opposition to all-day kindergarten in Rosedale. At a day-long conference on the all-day kindergarten in November, Dr. Blake told an audience of school administrators from other districts about the Extended Morning Program in Rosedale and his lack of support for an all-day kindergarten. He described the extended morning format as a compromise solution. He told the group that he had recommended it and the formation of an Ad Hoc Committee to the school board in order to resolve the disagreement between the principal and himself. He was against the all-day kindergarten concept, he said, because the Rosedale School Board did not support it, because the community had not had time to become familiar with it, and because he felt it was an issue that had little importance in a community like Rosedale where more than half of the residents did not have children in the schools. Thus, he said, a full-day kindergarten (which he estimated would cost close to $40,000) was bound to run into opposition until the need was strongly articulated in the community as well as in the school. He told the audience that day and reiterated to me in an interview several months later that he felt the district would eventually move to all-day kindergarten.

Developing an Evaluation Plan

Barbara Thornton perceived the Extended Morning Program as a first step toward an all-day kindergarten. She was committed to evaluating it to prove the value of additional time. The evaluation she envisioned was to involve testing, classroom observation, development of an evaluation plan, and communication with parents. She was emphatic about presenting the board and the community with "hard data," meaning standardized test scores, on the new program. She intended the evaluation to be a year-end report on the kindergarten to the superintendent and the school board.

Testing was done throughout the year. In late September and early October, the children were given the Brigance Test (1982). It was described to parents as a diagnostic screening by the kindergarten teachers. The test is designed to assess children's knowledge of letters, numbers, shapes, colors, and sound–symbol relationships. The first grade level of the test was used for all but two children; the kindergarten level was deemed "too easy." Within two weeks of the diagnostic screening, the children were given the Boehm Test (1970). In January, the children were given the TOBE (Test of Basic Experiences, Moss, 1979). In February, all were screened prior to commencement of work with the perceptual/motor training materials. In late April and early May, the kindergartners, along with the rest of the school, took the CTBS (1985) (California Test of Basic Skills) and, once again, they took the Boehm Test. All of these tests were paper and pencil instruments.

At no point during the school year was there an attempt to conduct a systematic developmental screening of the kindergarten children. Information on individual children's large and small motor skills, learning style, or readiness for paper and pencil work was gathered from classroom observations and, occasionally, from the written comments made by observers at the prior spring's kindergarten screening.

With the exception of the administration of the Brigance Test (1982), parents were not involved in the school's testing program. For the Brigance, parents brought their children back to school after lunch for a half-hour testing session with the child's teacher. Parents were invited into their child's classroom after the testing to meet with the teacher and discuss the screening instrument. Since no plans had been made to occupy the parents during the time that their children were being screened, I set up a reception area for them outside the kindergarten classrooms. My conversations with the parents during the screenings gave both me and the kindergarten faculty considerable information about the kindergarten class and about the parents' reactions to the new program.

I found that 93% of the class had attended preschool; 79% for two or more years. Their parents were generally in favor of the extended day program. They reported that their children came home happy and excited by a variety of school activities. Several parents pointed out that the extended day was no longer than that to which their children had been exposed in preschool. None of the parents reported that their children seemed tired when they got home from school. In fact, most of the children, I learned, participated in planned activities one or two afternoons per week. These included library story hour, art programs, gymnastics, eurhythmics, and afternoon classes designed specifically for kindergarten children at local nursery schools.

During the autumn, teachers and parents had two formal opportunities to share perceptions of the new kindergarten program. The first was "Back to School Night," held in early October. Second were the November parent–teacher conferences.

Early in November, I shared with the principal a proposed format for the evaluation. My plan focused on gaining feedback on the program from children, teachers, administrators, and parents. The children's reactions would be assessed through conversations with children and classroom observation by teachers and me. Reactions of parents, teachers, and administrators would be ascertained through questionnaires and interviews.

During the rest of November and December, the evaluation plan was refined. The principal met with all three kindergarten teachers on November 15. Together they developed a statement of goals and objectives for the program. In December, the principal and I began designing a questionnaire to ascertain the kindergarten parents' response to the new program. By early January, both the evaluation plan and the questionnaire were ready. At that point, I decided against developing a questionnaire to be given to the three kindergarten teachers and the principal. Our daily contact and their openness with me obviated the need for it.

Meanwhile . . . the Ad Hoc Committee Goes to Work

At the time that the school was involved in implementing and developing an evaluation of the Extended Morning Program, the Ad Hoc Committee to Study the Kindergarten had begun to meet and to work toward the production of a report for the school board due by March 1. At its first meeting in October, the committee reviewed its charges from the board to study the current kindergarten program in terms of the following options:

- Remaining with an extended morning program
- Reverting to a half-day program
- Instituting a full-day, call-back program
- Instituting a full-day, every day program
- Instituting another alternative

The parameters of their work were defined for them by the Board of Education's charges and by the chairperson: Their focus was to be solidly on the kindergarten program and development of a set of recommendations. Issues of day care and child care were, according to the chairperson, not within the purview of the committee.

Almost simultaneously, however, the day care/child care issue was being raised: At the November school board meeting, the chairperson of the Rosedale Community Education Program, a Board of Education sponsored group, outlined an after-school program for Rosedale children that her group hoped to implement in the elementary school during the next school year. The program would run both before and after school in one of the school's empty classrooms. The chairperson reported that responses to a questionnaire published in the district newsletter during the summer and parental inquiries indicated a need in the community for after-school child care. The program was to be modeled on similar programs in neighboring districts and would be supported by fees charged to those families that used it. The school board encouraged the group to send another questionnaire out to the community and to develop their plans in greater detail. They did both. In May, their proposal was accepted by the board. It went into effect the following autumn.

During their biweekly meetings between October and early January, the Ad Hoc Committee developed a schedule for their activities and formed into subcommittees that would study and report to the larger group on different aspects of the kindergarten issue. During these early meetings, the Ad Hoc Committee set the agenda for their report. They reviewed the principal's questionnaire from the prior January and her presentations at the March meetings. They familiarized themselves with the curriculum and schedule of the Extended Morning Kindergarten Program. They decided to visit those all-day kindergarten programs in the area that had not been visited by Doris Cohen and Barbara Thornton the previous year. Questionnaires and checklists to be used during these visits were developed and approved by the group. As many members as could were encouraged to observe in the Rosedale kindergarten. A small group was delegated to interview the principal and the kindergarten teachers regarding the new program. The Ad Hoc Committee decided against development of a community or parent questionnaire on all-day kindergarten.

Although they seemed hardly noteworthy at the time, several of the meetings that members of the Ad Hoc Committee initiated in November and December were to have a major impact of the outcome of the committee's work and the all-day kindergarten initiative in Rosedale. The first of these was held in November when several members of the Ad Hoc Committee came to the school to talk with the principal about the Extended Morning Program and to look over the parent questionnaire that we had prepared. A second set came in December and January when small groups of committee members observed in the three kindergarten classes. A third set involved two conversations, one in December and one in January, between the chairperson and the principal regarding the committee's work. The fourth was an interview conducted in January by a subcommittee of two parents who interviewed Doris Cohen and Ruth Fletcher at the home of one of the parents.

Concerned by questions that were raised in these various interviews and conversations by Ad Hoc Committee members about the duties of the full-time kindergarten teacher, Barbara Thornton not only developed a questionnaire to assess parental reaction to the Extended Morning Program but also began work on her own on a proposal for a limited call-back program. Barbara Thornton's action was prompted by her concern for Doris Cohen's position. Reasoning that she could not bring her concerns to the attention of the Ad Hoc Committee, she decided to develop a plan that would make the full-time kindergarten position secure. Her plan entailed keeping a small group of children on two afternoons each week for intensive work with the full-time kindergarten teacher. She asked me for any information that I might have on the effects of early intervention. She did not want any material that was based on research on programs for low-SES children.

CONFRONTATION

The kindergarten parent questionnaire and Barbara Thornton's plan for a limited call-back program provoked a confrontation between the school and the Ad Hoc Committee that ultimately changed the nature of the interactions among the school, the Ad Hoc Committee, and the school board.

The School Shapes a Plan

As a courtesy to the Ad Hoc Committee, Barbara Thornton released a copy of the proposed kindergarten parent questionnaire to the chairperson for committee review at their January 5 meeting. Committee reaction was uniformly negative. Members suggested items that they thought important to include in it, considered taking it to the Board of Education to prevent its use, and proposed a variety of alternatives. One of these was to have committee members interview all the kindergarten parents by telephone. It was finally decided that the chairperson would tell the principal about the committee's reactions and request that the committee be allowed to attach a page of their own questions to the questionnaire.

Barbara Thornton and I discussed the committee's reaction on the morning following the meeting. Later that day, Mrs. Thornton met with the superintendent to discuss the questionnaire. They decided to seek an independent evaluation of the questionnaire and to present the school's evaluation plan to the school board in executive session the following week. They reasoned that the questionnaire's importance as a critical element of the overall evaluation of the Extended Morning Kindergarten would then be obvious.

When the Board of Education met in executive session on January 9, the school's evaluation plan and the questionnaire were reviewed and approved. (The questionnaire was revised according to the suggestions of the outside reviewer and readied for the superintendent's approval on January 12. It was mailed to kindergarten parents on January 13.)

At the school board meeting, Barbara Thornton presented her proposal for a limited call-back program. She stressed two points: (1) the importance of early intervention and (2) the responsibility of educators to provide the necessary help when they have the resources to do so. She pointed out that 10 children had been identified by the kindergarten teachers to be "academically at risk." She also pointed out that explicit in the appointment of a full-time kindergarten teacher during the first year of the Extended Morning Program was the expectation that the teacher would have teaching duties on several afternoons each week. Doris Cohen's experience and expertise in early childhood education, the principal argued, made her the obvious choice for implementing a program of early intervention. The proposal was unanimously approved by the board. It was understood by all that approval was given only for the current school year.

Following school board approval, Barbara Thornton met with the kindergarten teachers and helped them design the schedule and procedures for the new call-back program. They were cautioned not to discuss it publicly until after the questionnaires had been sent out and returned.

The Ad Hoc Committee Shapes Its Report

When the Ad Hoc Committee met again on January 18, both the questionnaire and the call-back program had been approved by the board. The committee was given three copies of the updated questionnaire to study, but it was clear that it was too late for changes. The committee was not told explicitly by the school board liaison of the decision to institute the call-back program. During the meeting, subcommittees reported on their investigations of research on all-day kindergarten and on an interview with the kindergarten teachers. Also during the meeting, the chairperson distributed a list of questions to be answered by each committee member. Their responses, they were told, would become the basis for the final report.

Both the report on the teacher interviews and the committee's responses to the list of questions are important to consider in some depth because they figured strongly in the shape of the committee's final report and in the subsequent interactions of the school and the committee.

The Report on the Teacher Interviews. Two members of the Ad Hoc Committee (both previously members of the small parent-pressure group formed the previous spring) interviewed the kindergarten teachers, Doris Cohen and Ruth Fletcher, on January 11. The interview was conducted at the home of one of the subcommittee members because of her child-care problems. The teachers had been given the interview questions prior to the meeting; they told me that they felt "secure" about them.

The interviewers and teachers had divergent opinions about what went on during the interview. In their version, presented at the Ad Hoc Committee meeting on January 18, the interviewers focused on the teachers' use of the additional hour and the teachers' evaluation of the new program. They said the teachers felt the Extended Morning Program provided a more relaxed classroom atmosphere and gave increased time for academics and socialization. They noted that reading could not be taught every day—just on days when an aide was present in the kindergarten class. The teachers, they said, felt that the Extended Morning Program offered little time for remediation for children with developmental delays, that it placed a strain on the many children who attend a second program in the afternoon, and that it created instability in the kindergarten staff because of the two .6 positions instead of three full-time positions. The interviewers said the kindergarten schedule did not permit time for all three of the teachers to meet together during the morning; they surmised that there was some resentment on the part of the two .6 teachers about the amount of time they had to spend planning after school.

On the day before the interview subcommittee's presentation to the Ad Hoc Committee, the teachers described the interview to me. They remembered it differently. They felt that one of the interviewers was very much against the longer day and that neither parent was well-informed about kindergarten in general and about the differences between the Extended Morning Program and the former half-day program, particularly with regard to the issues of time for children's play and staff planning.

The discrepancy between the two perceptions of the interview continued unresolved until long after the report of the Ad Hoc Committee was issued. After the committee's report was made public in March, the teachers complained that the interviewers' presentation had misrepresented them. As the teachers went through the Ad Hoc Committee's report point by point with Barbara and me in April, they again reiterated their feelings about being misrepresented; they felt that trust with the community had been broken.

The Chairperson's Questions. The January 18 meeting ended with the chairperson handing out the following set of questions that committee members were required to answer within a week:

1. What alternative would you choose at this point and why?
2. If you are unable to make a recommendation at this point, why?
3. Do you feel academic and social development have equal importance in a kindergarten program? If not, how would you rate them in importance?
4. Do you feel that a first-grade curriculum has a place in the kindergarten program? Describe.
5. If other than a half-day or the present program is the recommendation of the committee, do you feel that we should recommend a half-day alternative be offered to those parents that want one?
6. What importance do you place on the teachers being part-time or full-time? If you feel the teachers should be part-time only,

how would you suggest they be compensated for planning time, faculty meetings, parent conferences and testing?
7. What weight should we as a committee give to such factors as fatigue, transition to first grade, money/budget?

Committee members' written responses to the questions were copied and distributed to each of the members prior to their next meeting on January 31. It seemed to me, at the time, that the committee was on the verge of recommending some type of call-back program.

The chairperson did not share her own responses. The committee's responses can be summarized as follows:

- *Program length and type*
  Extended morning—7 members
  Full-day kindergarten—4 members
  Alternate day call-back program—4 members
  No preference—1 member
- *Staffing*
  All kindergarten teachers part-time—8 members
  All kindergarten teachers full-time—8 members
- *Cost* was the key issue cited over and over again by committee members. The need for compensation for extra time spent in activities like conferences and screening was mentioned by several. Three recommended that the team leader position have an extra stipend attached. Three of the four in favor of having full-time kindergarten teachers said they would support part-time arrangements and were willing to switch if budgetary concerns required it.
- *Curriculum* was an issue of general agreement. Academics and social concerns were deemed of equal importance, and the curriculum of the first grade should not impinge on the program of the kindergarten. Members expressed a desire that advanced children be given enrichment and that children experiencing difficulty should receive remediation. They shared the opinion that kindergarten is an important, even pivotal, year of school that serves as an introductory experience. Several of the respondents favored studying the curriculum of the kindergarten further before extending the day more.

- *Other issues* such as fatigue and transition to first grade were not problematic to committee members. Most felt that if the district went to a call-back or a full-day program, no alternative programs should be planned.

As the chairperson had predicted, the committee's responses to her questions became the basis of the final report.

The January 31 Meeting

The Ad Hoc Committee meeting of January 31 was crucial to the outcome of the committee's work. The meeting brought together all the various lines of inquiry that the subcommittees had been pursuing since late October. It began with a discussion of the chairperson's questionnaire followed by reports from the subcommittees and a discussion of the school's limited call-back program.

The curriculum subcommittee reported the potential impact of the Extended Morning Program on the curriculum of the rest of the elementary school to be minimal. The research subcommittee's review concluded that the case for a longer day was inconclusive and that the social effects of the longer day versus the shorter day could not be measured. Their review pointed out the importance of teachers, the advantages of early education for all children, and the benefits of small groupings with a consistent set of adults. The budget subcommittee, referring to their experience in the community, pointed out that the costs of staffing a full-day or call-back program were too great for the minimal position that the kindergarten occupied in the larger picture of the entire Rosedale school system.

The limited call-back program was explained by the school board liaison, who reiterated with great conviction the arguments that Barbara Thornton had made to the school board regarding the need to address problems and the importance of doing so when the resources are available. Several committee members appeared disturbed that the call-back decision had been made without consulting the committee. Their complaints and questions during the evening indicated a concern that the work of the committee had been rendered meaningless by the school's action. They were angry. They asked me to leave. The discussion continued for several hours after that. ("Interesting," I noted in my journal, "that they are angry with me and not [board liaison] who could have given them this information at the last meeting!")

The chairperson's summary of the January 31 meeting covered two topics that were not discussed when I was present. The first of these was day care: She reported that since only 40 of the 60 questionnaires returned from the Rosedale Community Education survey showed an interest in day care, it was clear that this was not an issue! The second topic was a call for preparation for writing the final report. Committee members were asked to be ready with their own evaluations of the Extended Morning Program, to consider alternatives, and to determine what areas might require further study by the committee.

The school's failure to include the committee in the decision to implement the limited call-back program, coupled with its prior decision to send out the extended day parent questionnaire without committee approval, was to have a major impact on the Ad Hoc Committee's final report.

OUTCOME

The Ad Hoc Committee Report

Following the January 31 Ad Hoc Committee meeting, two more committee meetings were held. Toward the end of February, individual committee members met more frequently with the chairperson to prepare the final report. I was not invited to participate in these meetings. The report was made available to the superintendent, the principal, and the board early in March.

During February and early March, the key issue for the teachers and the principal was how to staff for the coming year. It was acknowledged by all in the school that the school board's decision regarding length of the kindergarten day would have major implications for staffing in the next school year. If the board recommended anything but a call-back or full-day program, the principal would have to excess the new part-time kindergarten teacher and move Doris Cohen to a part-time slot. The full-time position in the kindergarten would go to a teacher from an upper grade who would be transferred to the kindergarten. The teachers were all aware of this possibility. In conversations with me, they evidenced their concerns about job security and repeatedly expressed hope that the Ad Hoc Committee would recommend a call-back or full-day program.

On March 9, Mrs. Thornton announced that she had decided to retire at the end of the school year. She did not give her reasons. Many times during the course of the year, she had remarked to me on her growing weariness with the constant fighting with the school board and the difficulties of trying to please everyone, but I had not anticipated this. The teachers, especially the kindergarten teachers, were deeply upset. As they expressed it to me over the next few days, they were afraid for the future of the school in general, and for the kindergarten program in particular. The kindergarten teachers felt a loss of support. Doris Cohen described herself as "alone" and "vulnerable."

Barbara Thornton continued to lobby for a program that would require three full-time kindergarten teachers; but, during the spring, it became clear to the kindergarten teachers, particularly Doris Cohen, that the future direction of the kindergarten would have to be negotiated between the teachers and the superintendent.

The Ad Hoc Committee made its report to the school board and the superintendent on the evening of March 14 at an open school board meeting. In the afternoon, Ted Blake met with the kindergarten teachers and described the report to them. He left them with the admonition to think about other options besides a full-time program or a call-back program. They talked with other teachers in the school and with Mrs. Thornton and agreed that there would be no response from the teachers during the school board meeting.

All the Rosedale elementary school teachers were in attendance that evening. So, too, were all the Ad Hoc Committee members and many kindergarten parents. As they had agreed, the teachers did not comment on the report during the board meeting. There were few questions from the parents in the audience. Two Ad Hoc Committee members who espoused the minority opinion (they recommended a call-back program) stood to express their concern that the report did not make the minority opinion clear.

The Ad Hoc Committee recommended to the superintendent and the board that the Extended Morning Program be continued for the next year or two and that the following adjustments be made to the present program:

1. Present remediation programs at Rosedale Elementary School should be expanded to include kindergarten.

2. Individual testing should be done in September and October in the course of the regular school day. This would eliminate the cost incurred by afternoon testing and conferences in the 1982–1983 school year. Conferences, unless considered necessary by the parent or teacher, should be scheduled on Election Day consistent with the rest of the school.

3. The program should be staffed with three .7 teachers.
   - All teachers would work the same hours (8:15–1:09).
   - The additional time (one hour) after the children leave could be utilized by all three teachers for grade level planning and parent conferences.
   - Team leader stipend to be paid as on other grade levels.

4. The program would be staffed with three aides. An aide in each class each day would offer the following advantages:
   - Teachers would be free to teach reading and reading readiness each day.
   - Teachers would have the flexibility to address the individual needs of the class.
   - Scheduling of specials at the same time for all kindergarten classes, followed by snack time with the aide, would provide a 50-minute block of time for each of the teachers. This could be used as grade level planning time for the teachers or give them the opportunity to meet with individual or small groups of children for enrichment, remediation, or testing activities.

5. Following the above recommendations would set the cost of the kindergarten program at $87,940, a savings of $4,739. This money should be applied to further development of the kindergarten curriculum and program.

With the publication of the report, the Ad Hoc Committee was dissolved. The members were never called upon as a group to articulate or defend the position that they had finally taken. The report stood as the summation of their work. Expression of the parental viewpoint regarding the kindergarten program reverted to the community.

The School's Response to the Report

In the weeks after the presentation of the Ad Hoc Committee report, the school mobilized its energies to counteract it. The teachers met with the principal to draw up a list of the report's inaccuracies. These, along with a memo from the principal stating her opinion of the problems inherent in the staffing recommended by the Ad Hoc Committee, were submitted to the superintendent on April 7. The school's report on the Extended Morning Kindergarten went into full gear. Barbara felt that the only way to counteract the Ad Hoc Committee report was to provide the superintendent and the board with substantive information. The success of the school's effort would be determined, she and the teachers knew, by the final recommendation of the school board.

I met with each of the kindergarten teachers to discuss their reactions to the program. Their responses were incorporated into the school's evaluation that was submitted to the superintendent and the board on April 15. On April 7, at a regularly scheduled staff meeting, the principal projected staffing patterns two years ahead. She based her projections on the Ad Hoc Committee's recommendation of three part-time positions in the kindergarten. All the elementary school teachers stayed after the meeting to discuss the kindergarten problem and to draft a letter to the superintendent in which they demanded three full-time kindergarten teachers for the coming year. Prior to the meeting, Doris Cohen went to talk with the superintendent and insisted that the kindergarten have at least one full-time person even if that person was inexperienced.

Kindergarten parents and parents of older children in the school also mobilized their energies to respond to the Ad Hoc Committee report. The director of a local nursery school reacted with alarm to the prospect of a kindergarten program staffed by part-time people untrained in early childhood. She notified the parents of children in her school and asked them to attend the April 11 school board meeting to voice their concerns. Other parents met informally and agreed on a statement that they would make at the school board meeting.

The turnout at the April 11 school board meeting was almost twice that of the March 14 meeting. Parents were there in large numbers. The elementary school teachers had been sent reminders earlier in the day asking them to attend. The school board appeared surprised by the large turnout: There was no item on the agenda that provided the audience with a platform for their comments. Not until the end of the meeting did the audience have a chance to talk. At that time, leaders of teacher and parent groups made their presentations.

The feeling expressed by many both during and after the meeting was that their arguments were futile. They felt that the board had already made its decision based on the recommendations of the Ad Hoc Committee. They perceived the board to be indifferent, even hostile. The teachers and principal were rankled by the board's publication, subsequent to the March 14 meeting, of excerpts of the Ad Hoc Committee report in the district newsletter. The principal felt that its publication gave it unwarranted importance. The teachers felt that its publication took the kindergarten issue out of their hands.

Barbara Thornton did not learn until March 30, in conversation with the superintendent, that, convinced by her concern about the problems of a kindergarten program staffed by part-time people, he had attempted to put salaries for three full-time kindergarten teachers into the budget. In executive session with the board, his plan was rejected. The board, he told the principal, was unanimous in its support of the Ad Hoc Committee's recommendations, particularly the recommendation for three .7 positions and three aides. The superintendent found himself isolated in his interactions with the school board on the kindergarten issue. Although Ted Blake had reserved for himself the right to make the final recommendation on the kindergarten staffing (which he did at the May 2 school board meeting), he opted not to oppose the board. Instead, he prepared to reassign teachers and to lay off the part-time kindergarten teachers and Doris Cohen.

On April 18, the eve of spring vacation, the superintendent issued a letter to the entire district in which he explained the problems regarding staffing and the kindergarten. Doris Cohen went to talk with him. She was despondent. She had fought earlier in the week with Barbara Thornton about a list of questions that Mrs. Thornton had submitted to the kindergarten teachers that required their making quantitative comparisons of the performance of current kindergartners with that of the previous year's students. The teachers had been irate. Doris Cohen felt the questions were "insulting," but she and the others had bowed to the principal's request, convinced by the argument that "hard data" were the only thing the school board would heed. Now, they felt there was no hope.

On April 19, Ted Blake received the principal's recommendation regarding kindergarten staffing. Barbara Thornton recommended three full-time positions and a gradual phase-in of an alternate day call-back program. On the same day, the board received the school's evaluation of the Extended Morning Kindergarten Program. In it, the principal stressed, as evidence of the program's efficacy, positive feedback from parents and teachers, children's clear comfort with the new schedule, and significant achievement gains made by current kindergartners in comparison with children who had been in the half-day program the previous year.

The School Board's Decision

At the May 2 school board meeting, Ted Blake made his formal recommendation that the kindergarten be staffed by one full-time, two part-time (.7) teachers, and two aides during the coming year. Board members' questions and comments that evening convinced the principal, the teachers, and those parents who sided with them in their battle for a full-day program that financial considerations played a key role in the board's attitude toward the kindergarten issue. The board echoed the Ad Hoc Committee's contention that the extra expenditure entailed by a longer day and full-time staff was disproportionate to the overall needs of the district. Further, their comments during the meetings of March 14, April 11, and May 2 indicated that their reluctance to spend money on the kindergarten program was due, in part, to skepticism regarding the role of schools in early childhood education: "Kindergarten," one female board member remarked, "should be part with mommy and part with school." Board members questioned the substantial academic gains claimed for the current kindergarten class in the principal's evaluation. Barbara Thornton's focus on academic gains appeared to clash with the board's understanding that the kindergarten program was strong to begin with, that the original proposal for the extended morning was for enrichment, and that testing in the kindergarten was done not for evaluation but only for diagnostic purposes.

The final phase of the school's evaluation of the program came with the CTBS tests in May. The teachers were pleased with the children's relaxation and lack of concern when taking the tests in comparison with the previous kindergarten groups with whom they had worked. They attributed the children's attitude to the relaxed pace of the Extended Morning Program. The principal asked me to hand score the tests and to compare the results with those of the previous year.

She said that she was convinced that there would be substantial gains in the scores of the current group over those of the previous year. Here again, Mrs. Thornton's insistence on "hard data" clashed with the kindergarten teachers' methods of evaluation.

The test results showed that the scores of the current kindergarten class were higher in all categories than those of the previous kindergarten class, which had also taken the CTBS test at the end of their kindergarten year. It was not clear, however, that the improvement was due to the new schedule; hence, the test scores did not figure prominently in the subsequent decision making about the kindergarten program.

The superintendent's recommendation that the kindergarten be staffed by one full-time, two part-time (.7) teachers, and two aides during the coming year did not solve the kindergarten staffing problems. Declining enrollments required changes in staffing of upper grades. In accordance with union agreements, the two part-time positions in the kindergarten became available to the least senior of the tenured faculty. On May 18, Doris Cohen was notified by the superintendent that she had the option of taking a part-time position in the kindergarten or of leaving Rosedale altogether. She and the other kindergarten teachers were very dispirited. For most of the school year, they had been aware that their jobs were in jeopardy. But, until the Ad Hoc Committee report on March 14, they had been hopeful that a call-back program would be initiated and that they would remain on the staff as full-time teachers. After the committee report, their morale had deteriorated significantly.

By May 31, all three kindergarten teachers had been reinstated. An elementary teacher had announced plans to leave the school. As a result, there would be no changes in the kindergarten personnel. Among the kindergarten teachers, I wrote in my journal, there was "no hoopla or fanfare; there was no joy about it from anyone." Within another week, the situation changed again. Another elementary school teacher announced plans to leave. Ruth Fletcher was reassigned from her part-time kindergarten position to a full-time position on an upper grade level. Once again the kindergarten was vulnerable.

The board's decision came in July. It approved continuation of the Extended Morning Kindergarten Program staffed by one full-time kindergarten teacher and two part-time (.6) teachers. By the time school opened in September, it was clear that there would be another change in the kindergarten staff. In October, Donna Weaver was reassigned to an upper grade. For the fifth year in a row, Doris Cohen had a new staff to train.

Now, almost 10 years later, Rosedale still maintains an extended morning kindergarten program and a parent-supported after-school program. There appears to be no need for all-day kindergarten.

CHAPTER 5

Kindergarten Planning in Middle City

This chapter describes the development of a plan to implement all-day kindergarten in a small city that I have named Middle City. The story concludes with a brief description of an implementation of an extended morning kindergarten program. The chapter is designed to give the reader a sense of how consultants can work with schools in the initiation and implementation of early childhood programs.

A suburb of a large city, Middle City is itself a racially and economically diverse small city with a public school system serving 7,700 students—2,200 of whom are in the city's high school. The Middle City public schools provide a wide range of programs. These include a pre-kindergarten program, five elementary schools (one of which is a magnet school focused on the humanities), two middle schools, and a comprehensive high school that provides college preparatory programs and business and vocational education. Parent participation is encouraged through strong PTA organizations in each of the city's schools and other school-sponsored activities.

For many years, Middle City has been a proving ground for innovations, particularly those relating to racial equity. The racial and ethnic diversity that characterizes the city and its school system has been achieved through careful planning and concerted effort on the part of the City Council and the school board.

During the school year under study, the Middle City schools were facing the following problems: increasing racial isolation of the Hispanic and low-income African-American communities, with the concomitant problem of racial balance of the city's schools; declining enrollments in some of the city's schools coupled with burgeoning enrollments in others; a need for more space and enhanced facilities; and declining state funding. A demographic study, in progress at the time, had been commissioned by the school board to provide critical information for long-range planning.

GETTING STARTED

The all-day kindergarten initiative in Middle City began with a small group of kindergarten teachers. Very early in their discussions, they involved the district office and other kindergarten teachers from each of the city's elementary schools. This inclusiveness was to characterize the planning process in Middle City from here on.

The Teachers' Study Committee

The kindergarten teachers who initiated the discussion of all-day kindergarten in Middle City met with the Assistant Superintendent for Elementary Education, Bob Flowers, early in the spring and, with his help, developed a committee of kindergarten teachers representing each of the city's elementary schools to study the feasibility of all-day kindergarten in Middle City. The Kindergarten Study Committee set themselves the following tasks:

1. Develop a philosophy for all-day kindergarten
2. Assess the need for district-wide, all-day kindergarten
3. Review the present kindergarten curriculum
4. Design a developmentally appropriate all-day kindergarten program; include first-grade teachers in planning
5. Inventory current materials/equipment and project needs for a new program
6. Visit existing all-day programs
7. Engage parents in planning

By the end of June, the committee had accomplished a significant portion of its task list: They had developed a philosophy and goals, reviewed the current kindergarten curriculum, and visited a variety of all-day programs. Over the summer, they reviewed research on all-day kindergarten and finalized a report on all-day kindergarten for distribution in the fall as a working paper. The report included their philosophy, a needs assessment, materials inventory, time line for further study and planning, and references. The committee gave themselves a year to get ready to implement district-wide, all-day kindergarten.

The Kindergarten Task Force

In September, Dr. Flowers invited broader participation in the all-day kindergarten issue through formation of a district-wide task force to further study and plan for all-day kindergarten in Middle City. The task force would comprise the five elementary school principals; both teachers and parents from each of the elementary schools' pre-kindergarten, kindergarten, and first-grade programs; a Board of Education representative; and representatives from the community at large. Each of the elementary schools was asked to submit a list of participants.

Having become sensitive, through observation of the experiences of neighboring school districts, to the difficulties of implementing all-day kindergarten, Dr. Flowers decided to work with consultants on the project. He contacted Dr. Burton Baxter, who had worked closely in the past with the Middle City school district on a variety of issues related to desegregation and equity. Knowing me and my research on the initiation and implementation of all-day kindergarten programs, Dr. Baxter suggested that I be contacted as a second facilitator working with the All-Day Kindergarten Task Force.

The first All-Day Kindergarten Task Force meeting in October was tightly planned. We anticipated approximately 60 attendees—principals, early childhood teachers, and parent representatives from each of the five elementary schools in the district; 150 people turned out. As we surveyed the group and talked with individuals before the meeting began, we were surprised and concerned by an apparent lack of minority representation: Despite the district office efforts to ensure broad representation, there were few African-Americans and Hispanics.

The meeting began with an introduction by Dr. Flowers in which he described the work done over the summer by the Kindergarten Study Committee, outlined the structure of the task force, and set the end of January—only three months away—as the deadline for the task force's work. He laid out for the group a set of parameters that Dr. Baxter and I had developed with him to guide their work. These were

1. Awareness of the long-range goals of the district
2. Attention to the implications of demographic studies of the district for their planning

3. Attention to early childhood research
4. Impact of a new program on the magnet school
5. The need to reduce minority isolation in the school district

At my suggestion, Dr. Flowers distributed copies of the working paper of the Kindergarten Study Committee and made copies of the following books available to the group: Fromberg's *The Full-Day Kindergarten* (1987), Katz and Chard's *Engaging Children's Minds: The Project Approach* (1989), and Warger's *A Resource Guide to Public School Early Childhood Programs* (1988). He stressed community participation in the task force, describing the work of this group as a "major opportunity for community input."

Before Dr. Baxter could follow, there were questions from the audience concerning

- The status of the pre-kindergarten program: Dr. Flowers assured them that it would be maintained.
- The possibility of a call-back program because, the questioner said, it would be cheaper: Dr. Flowers disagreed about the cost but said that the format was a possibility as were others.
- The location of a district-wide, all-day kindergarten program: Dr. Flowers referred to his introduction and reminded them that this would be one of the recommendations.

Repeatedly throughout Dr. Flowers's presentation, there were interruptions and questions about the viability of the task force's work. These appeared to be motivated by concern that district-wide, all-day kindergarten had already been decided on. Dr. Flowers repeatedly assured the group that a decision about all-day kindergarten would not be made by the school board until the task force had completed its work and made its recommendation.

Following Bob Flowers's introductory remarks, Dr. Baxter led off with an overview of the process that the task force would be following and provided the group with an organizational framework and time line. He described for them a process that we designed by which the task force group would be divided into subcommittees to address the following areas: curriculum, parent involvement, staffing and staff development, organization, physical plant (including location of the program and transportation), and screening, including testing and reporting. He

listed six meeting dates—two per month before the end of January—
and outlined the Task Force's charges. I followed with a description
of the organization and tasks of each subcommittee.

When we finished, questions for Dr. Flowers began again.

- Why change the kindergarten schedule?
- What do these committees mean?
- Don't we need more time before we start forming committees?
- Is all-day kindergarten already a foregone conclusion?

Dr. Flowers responded briefly but substantively to each question,
referring where he could to his earlier remarks and the materials that
had been made available to the group. Within the hour, the audience
of 150 had chosen subcommittees and left the hall in which we were
meeting for smaller meeting rooms throughout the building.

Each subcommittee was supposed to include a school administrator, a kindergarten or preschool teacher, a parent, and, when possible,
a first-grade teacher. No subcommittee was to have a majority of members from any one of the district's five elementary schools. At its first
meeting, each subcommittee designated its own chair and recorder and
determined its own meeting format. School administrators were asked
not to assume leadership roles in the subcommittees. Dr. Baxter and I
moved among the subcommittees that first evening, noting their size
and makeup and, where necessary, helping to clarify their task. We
noted that the organization and the staffing and staff development subcommittees were larger than the others. We encouraged participants in
both groups to move to other subcommittees, and we followed up on
this when the whole group reassembled at the end of the evening.

THE PROCESS

Dr. Baxter and I had designed our work with the All-Day Kindergarten Task Force to promote communication among all of the task
force members and to provide for individual input in the decision-
making process. Each meeting, therefore, was scheduled from 7:30–
10 in the evening and was divided into both small group and large group
sessions. We anticipated having six meetings with the group. At the
beginning of the first three meetings, we planned for presentations on

critical topics for the task force: research on early childhood education
(I would do that one), the issue of minority isolation in the district (to
be addressed by a member of the superintendent's staff), and reports
on visits to all-day kindergarten programs (to be conducted by one of
the kindergarten teachers). These presentations were to be approximately
20 minutes and would be followed immediately by subcommittee work
and reporting out to the entire task force at 9:30. After each meeting,
the subcommittees were to submit a progress report to the facilitators.
These would be typed and distributed to the whole group along with
the agenda at the next meeting. Because we were coming from other
settings to our work with the Middle City All-Day Kindergarten Task
Force, Dr. Baxter and I planned to debrief with each other after each
meeting and to include Dr. Flowers whenever possible.

Meeting 2, Early November

As on the first evening, attendance at the second meeting was high.
The meeting began with a short talk by Bob Flowers focusing on the
need for patience with the process. He emphasized that he knew that
the development of all-day kindergarten in the district would take time.
He had stressed this with the board, he told the group. Again, there
were questions about site—one or several?—and about demographic
factors affecting long-range planning in the district. Again, Dr. Flowers reiterated the district's commitment to the work of the task force
and his willingness to provide them with whatever information they
needed for their work. Dr. Baxter followed Dr. Flowers with the
evening's agenda, a reminder about the focus of each of the subcommittees, and a request that there be broad representation on each
subcommittee, including school people, parents, and the general community. Since the membership of the various subcommittees was still
fluid at this point, Dr. Baxter encouraged task force participants (with
the exception of the five principals, each of whom had decided on a
subcommittee focus ahead of time) to move to other subcommittees.
Dr. Baxter's suggestion was aimed at evening out the number of participants in each subcommittee, particularly the organization and the
staffing and staff development subcommittees, which, as we had noted
at the first meeting, appeared to be larger than the others. Then I gave
a brief presentation of the research on all-day kindergarten, laying out
as clearly as I could a description of the five-year-old child, the con-

cept of developmentally appropriate practice, and the implications of the research for development of kindergarten programs and curriculum.

As we moved among the various subcommittees that evening, Dr. Baxter and I noted several things: The size of the subcommittees had evened out; they seemed smaller than they had been two weeks before, now averaging about 15 members to a subcommittee; and quite a number of individuals had done considerable homework in the time since the first meeting. We discovered later that a number of individuals had come just for the opening session and had left when the task force group broke into the various subcommittees.

By the end of the second meeting, the subcommittees had begun to move toward consensus on a variety of critical issues. In the reporting-out session at the end of the evening, it was clear that the process that we had developed was working: The subcommittees were engaged in substantive discussion of their respective topics; they seemed to understand that the process was designed to help them produce a final report.

1. The curriculum committee had decided that the curriculum of an all-day kindergarten should not be "watered down first grade." They were unanimous in the conviction that the kindergarten year should be unpressured, allowing children freedom to explore and to make mistakes.
2. The staffing committee had developed a list of objectives and priorities.
3. The organization committee had begun by working on the idea of kindergarten in one facility and was realizing that there were other options. They identified the issues of space and money as key to any decision that the district might make.
4. After comparing a variety of screening instruments and viewing a videotape on developmental readiness, the screening committee decided that teacher involvement in kindergarten screening was essential and that all children should be screened. They planned to see what other school districts were doing on this topic. They were beginning to focus on what types of information are gained from screenings and how that information is used.
5. The parent involvement committee considered ways to involve parents that would acknowledge the diverse needs of parents in Middle City.

6. The subcommittee charged with the physical plant reported initial confusion about their task, so they had spent their time reviewing the working paper of the Kindergarten Study Committee. There was general consensus in the group with the suggestions in the working paper. The subcommittee members were planning on moving to topics such as transportation and consideration of the layout of existing facilities in the district.

In our debriefing session at the end of the evening, Dr. Flowers, Dr. Baxter, and I discussed the fact that the subcommittees were working well and that each had found an abundance of essential issues in their areas to address over the next weeks. Dr. Baxter and I were pleased by the subcommittees' progress; Dr. Flowers worried about their momentum. He seemed anxious and wary of a group process whose outcome was unpredictable. Dr. Baxter and I were committed to giving the groups time to develop a feeling of expertise in their respective areas. We were just beginning to see this happen. We envisioned at least one and perhaps two more meetings devoted to the small group work of the subcommittees.

Meeting 3, Mid-November

One week later, the task force met again. The meeting began with approximately 40 people—significantly fewer people than had been at the two earlier meetings. By 8:00, the size of the group had grown to about 60, but it was never again the hundred or so individuals that it had been during the first two meetings.

This third meeting began with a presentation by a member of the superintendent's staff on the issue of minority isolation and demographic trends in the district. Her presentation lasted approximately 10 minutes and was followed by questions from the task force audience.

- Is a second magnet school being considered?
- What are the options being considered for the reduction of minority isolation?
- What could be done to prevent minority isolation?
- What is the role of the demographer?
- Isn't all-day kindergarten a luxury, given the circumstances of the district?

These were important questions touching on sensitive issues that got to the heart of the district's organization and commitment to racial balance in the city's schools. While Dr. Flowers acknowledged the importance of the issue of minority isolation, he stressed his conviction that all-day kindergarten was a program that could benefit all the children of the district, not just a small group.

Dr. Baxter and I had arranged for a second large group presentation that evening on staffing arrangements for all-day kindergarten. The presentation was made by the chairperson of the staffing and staff development subcommittee. The subcommittee had made a decision not to consider any staffing options except staffing for all-day kindergarten. Members of the subcommittee had contacted neighboring districts that had all-day programs to see how they had handled the staffing issue. The report focused exclusively on staffing arrangements; no mention was made of staff development.

Dr. Baxter then took over and focused the subcommittees on developing rationales for their work and identifying one or two things that they really wanted to concentrate on for the final report. He told them that they would have slightly less time for their small group work that evening so that the reporting-out session could be extended. (He and I and Dr. Flowers were becoming concerned about how quickly time was passing. We wanted to make sure that the final report would contain the substantive materials necessary for the superintendent's and school board's decision.)

The reporting-out session was lengthy. Each subcommittee took time to present a summary of its deliberations to the entire group:

1. The curriculum committee described a developmentally appropriate, success-oriented, unpressured program in which there would be community involvement and time for experimentation and small group work.
2. The organization committee raised questions that they wanted to turn over to the curriculum committee: What are the implications of class size? (They felt that 20 children with a teacher and a full-time teaching assistant was optimal.) Would there be substantial differences in curricula between neighborhood-based programs and a centrally located early childhood center? How does team teaching affect curriculum? To the staffing committee, they referred the question of staff development for team teaching and for a longer day.

3. The staffing committee came back with considerations of two staffing alternatives: an early childhood center approach using the Princeton Plan and a neighborhood school approach. For both, they felt it essential to develop an integrated, district-wide kindergarten program, so they, too, turned to the curriculum committee. They acknowledged that a center approach would necessitate considerable staffing changes depending on the number of children involved and the grade levels affected. They were ready to focus on these options and weigh their merits.

4. The parent involvement committee developed a set of topics to focus their work: parenting, communicating, volunteering, learning at home, and governing. Their report focused on what parents could do to help children learn better. There was no mention of the things that school personnel might do to support families of young children in the district.

5. Like the staffing subcommittee, the screening group had contacted other programs. They continued to voice their belief in universal informal screening for all kindergartners and the involvement of the kindergarten teachers in the screenings. They were moving toward identification of key developmental areas. They recommended that the findings from kindergarten screenings be used to plan an appropriate education for each child.

6. The subcommittee charged with the physical plant reported their consensus on the need to locate all-day kindergarten programs in neighborhood schools. As reasons they gave fewer changes for the children, proximity of siblings, availability of role models among older children, and ability to participate in the life of the school, for example, book and science fairs.

The meeting closed with remarks from Dr. Flowers, who thanked the group for their hard work and assured them that the controversial issues regarding site selection and availability (e. g., whether the program would be in one central facility or in neighborhood schools; whether the program would be available to all children in the district) that were beginning to emerge would be resolved as they were addressed by the entire task force over the next few meetings. However, in our debriefings that evening and over the next weeks, Dr. Flowers admitted that he was getting nervous. He had not anticipated the range of differences and the potential for a bitter dispute that was showing itself in the questions that were asked in the large group meetings and addressed to him in private. I was disappointed that it was only in the curriculum committee that I heard discussions of developmentally appropriate practice; yet I was heartened that individuals were talking openly in their small groups about their concerns about the need for full-day kindergarten, staffing, and site selection.

Over the next three weeks, Dr. Baxter and I developed a broad outline of the final report and a list of questions to guide the task force.

Meeting 4, Early December: Beginning the Final Report

By early December, task force members had gathered the information that they needed for their subcommittee recommendations. They had had time to argue through with one another the various perspectives that might be taken on their subcommittee topics. Dr. Baxter and I were prepared to begin a new level of work with them. We came to the meeting with an outline and draft of the final report that included the district's mission statement, the charges to the task force, a section on Considerations and Constraints, a preliminary review of the research on kindergarten and early education, and a section on Program Design in which we included the various subcommittee recommendations made thus far. Attached to the draft were the following 10 questions, which we wanted each subcommittee to consider:

1. *Population*: Who will attend the all-day kindergarten program?
2. *Screening:* How will children be selected for kindergarten? For first grade?
3. *Curriculum*: What should you teach children in kindergarten?
4. *Site selection*: Where will the program be housed?
5. *Facilities*: What kind of physical facilities are needed? Inside? Outside?
6. *Staffing and staff development*: Who will staff the program(s)? How will they be prepared and supported?
7. *Articulation*: How will the program relate to preschool education and elementary education in the district?
8. *Possible outcomes—evaluation*: What should children learn and be able to do when they leave kindergarten?
9. *Alternatives*: What skills should children have that will carry on into later education? How will the program achieve these goals?

10. *District outcomes*: What should be the impact of the program on the education of students in the Middle City schools?

While the individual subcommittees had provided answers to many of these questions, the entire task force had not had an opportunity to talk them through together. Our intent was to stimulate that discussion. We reasoned that it was, after all, to be their report and recommendations that would be given to the school board and superintendent; it was they, not Dr. Baxter or I, who would have to live with the program that they would recommend; and it was they, not we, who would have to articulate the recommendations and their rationale to the community.

The meeting began with a report from one of the kindergarten teachers about a visit to an all-day kindergarten program. Dr. Flowers was not there so Dr. Baxter and I followed with the draft of the final report and the 10 questions listed above. We explained that each group was to address all of the questions. We allocated the next 45 minutes to the subcommittee meetings. Prior to the subcommittees' return, we taped blank sheets of newsprint on every available wall space around the hall. When they returned at 8:30, we asked each group to have its members fill in the newsprint giving the consensus of the group for each question. In short order, the newsprint was filled around the room with answers to questions 1–5 (most of the subcommittees had taken the questions in order and had only gotten that far). Then the reporting-out from the subcommittees began.

The response of the large group to this exercise was fascinating to us. We asked first for the reports of the subcommittees whose expertise was the focus of the question; thus, for example, the curriculum committee addressed question 3 first and the others followed. There was more unanimity than we had anticipated in the responses. Where there was a difference of opinion, it was not we, the consultants, but the subcommittees who addressed the issue. They, after all, had become the experts.

At this and the following meeting, these general discussions of each question produced a consensus, which Dr. Baxter and I used to fashion a statement on the issues that were the focus of each of the questions. These we brought back to the task force for consideration and comment early in January. They were accepted with few revisions, for, essentially, they represented the thinking of the entire task force.

Population and Screening. In brief, the task force recommended all-day kindergarten for all children in the district whose birthday occurs before December 31. Kindergarten screening, they felt, should be consistent throughout the district, with one informal screening in the spring before kindergarten and a formal screening in the fall to facilitate the development of appropriate curriculum and instruction. As a group, they were opposed to standardized testing of young children, wanted to see parent representation in the screening process, and hoped that all-day kindergarten would promote better articulation between kindergarten and first grade, with less pressure for children in both settings.

Curriculum. The curriculum group was joined by the rest of the task force members in recommending a developmentally appropriate format in which play is seen as the child's work and the activities of the kindergarten day are seen not as discrete events but as an interrelated set of experiences. The task force saw the strength of all-day as opposed to half-day kindergarten being the additional time it offers for enrichment and exploration.

Site Selection and Facilities. The issues of site selection and facilities were critical in the group's discussion that night and to the outcome of the final report. While the task force members were clear on the need for facilities specifically designed for the needs of young children, they were still divided on the issue of site selection. Many in the group advocated housing the program in a single early childhood center in which appropriate facilities were available. They admitted, however, that there was no school site in the district large enough to house such a program. The compromise reached that evening was to recommend that all-day kindergartens be housed in neighborhood schools, but the Final Report was to make clear the task force's willingness to consider alternatives if the Board of Education found implementation unfeasible in so many sites. They even developed a set of suggestions for the Board.

Meeting 5, Mid-December: The Second Set of Questions

A week later, we came together to address questions 6–10 and two additional questions that Dr. Baxter and I had developed.

11. What should be the role of parents in the all-day kindergarten program?
12. In light of the considerations and constraints, such as maintaining the district's objective of reducing minority isolation, what alternatives to the recommendations should be considered?

We gave the first hour to the subcommittees to develop their responses to these questions as well as those not addressed the previous week. Again, the reporting-out was done on newsprint in the large group, and once again we found ourselves facilitating a rich discussion among the subcommittees.

Staffing and Staff Development. The task force recommended a staffing ratio of 1:20 in the kindergarten, with a teaching assistant or aide for each classroom. They recommended parent involvement and staff development in early childhood practice for kindergarten and first-grade teachers and aides. They suggested opportunities for regular meetings among the kindergarten teachers and for observations of other all-day programs. They discussed the necessity of providing the same range of support services to the kindergarten program, irrespective of site, that were available to other school programs: ESL, special education, arts, custodial, nursing, social worker, lunchroom monitors, and so forth.

Articulation. Picking up on the site selection and facilities discussion of the previous week, they described the all-day kindergarten program as Phase I of an early childhood center program that would bring all of the district's early childhood programs—the pre-kindergarten program, kindergarten, and the primary grades—together in one or two facilities. They stressed the importance of the kindergarten year as part of a continuum in a young child's education. They envisioned an early childhood center or centers as optimal environments in which to facilitate broad communication among staff and between home and school.

Outcomes and Alternatives. The outcomes of an all-day kindergarten program anticipated by the task force fit with those claimed in the research on early childhood programs and all-day kindergarten: increased socialization, tolerance for diversity, high self-esteem and establishment of the disposition for lifelong learning, better communication skills, easier adaptation to school, greater home–school–community understanding, development of an outstanding early childhood teaching staff, and enhancement of the district's reputation and image.

Meeting 6, Early January

In the week following the December break, the task force met again to review our write-up of their recommendations and a draft of the final report that Dr. Baxter and I had developed during the holiday period. They quickly recognized the recommendations as theirs. They agreed with the statement on considerations and constraints. But they were not so sanguine with the rationale, which contained background on all-day kindergarten as well as on other early childhood programs; material on child development, the concept of developmentally appropriate practice, assessment in the kindergarten, and home–school relationships; and a summary that led into the task force recommendations. They worked together in small groups to formulate their concerns, then reported back to the large forum with their objections and sentence-by-sentence revisions. The rationale was revised, with key headings and topics added and the "tone" changed to better reflect the language and perspectives of the task force members.

By the end of the meeting, there was broad consensus on the preliminary document that we had presented to them that evening.

Meeting 7, End of January: The Final Report

The last meeting of the task force was brief. A full draft of the final report minus appendices was distributed. After a few minor corrections and a decision to eliminate the description of specific alternatives to their recommendations, the group overwhelmingly endorsed the report. It was, after all, theirs.

The discussion moved to the presentation of the report to the superintendent and the Board of Education. The key question before the group was who would represent the task force at that presentation. Reasoning that Dr. Flowers would be there anyway, and that the principals had other forums in which their opinions were solicited, the decision was made to choose one of the kindergarten teachers and two parents.

The All-Day Kindergarten Task Force had finished its work. After careful consideration of the needs of the children in the district and the district itself, they had unanimously recommended all-day kindergarten. They were comfortable with their recommendations about curriculum, staffing, parent involvement, equipment, and scheduling. They were concerned that the program might meet with difficulty if the problems of site(s), staffing, and support were not addressed by the board.

THE SCHOOL BOARD DECISION

Late in March, the designated task force members joined Dr. Baxter and me to present the recommendations of the All-Day Kindergarten Task Force at an executive session of the school board. A number of other committee members (parents, teachers, and administrators) appeared to hear our presentation and the board's response. The school board had been given copies of both the final report and an executive summary that briefly described the work of the task force and listed its recommendations.

Dr. Baxter began the presentation by briefly describing the task force, its charges, and the process that was followed. I took up the rationale. The kindergarten teacher addressed the curricular and programmatic issues inherent in the recommendations, and the parents focused on issues related to parent and community support. The presentation, which lasted approximately 20 minutes, was followed by questions from members of the board to the task force presenters. Comments from the floor were then solicited. One of the parents who spoke that night told the board members that she had been among those most adamantly opposed to the issue of all-day kindergarten at the early task force meetings. She told them that her work with the task force had convinced her that all-day kindergarten was not only a good idea for Middle City, but was essential, and she urged the board to approve the adoption of district-wide, all-day kindergarten.

In May, the board decided against implementing district-wide, all-day kindergarten, claiming the constraints of cost and space—the two issues that the facilities subcommittee had identified as critical at the first task force meeting.

TRYING AN EXTENDED MORNING PROGRAM

During the summer following the school board's decision, the principal of the Calhoun School, one of the elementary schools in the district, decided to develop an extended morning kindergarten program in her school. With the support of the kindergarten teachers and the PTA, she approached the district office for approval, which was received. The program began early in November. It entailed a number of changes, the effects of which went beyond the kindergarten itself: (1) an additional hour of school for both the morning and afternoon kindergarten classes, (2) additional support staff assigned to the kindergarten programs during the transitional noon-time hour, and (3) changing the schedule of the school's arts programs to accommodate the new kindergarten schedule.

The kindergarten teachers worked with me, acting as a consultant, during the early fall months to prepare for the new program. They planned for enrichment activities—art, music, movement, second language instruction, computer—during the latter part of the kindergarten session for the morning students and during the first part of the session for the afternoon students. By putting these activities at the beginning or end of the session, they felt that they would have enough class time to allow for uninterrupted exploration, small group work, and projects.

Once the new program went into effect, I was to continue to meet with the teachers and their assistants to help them with curriculum and instruction. However, the schedule was the focus of their attention throughout the new program's early months: Providing time for the teachers' lunch hour and simultaneously ensuring a high-quality program proved to be enormously difficult. Schedules that had been developed for arts teachers throughout the school had to be revised; some were more amenable to change than others. First through fifth grade teachers who had developed their schedules had to change them; not all were willing to do so. The schedule became a source of friction between the kindergarten teachers and the principal; its fallout was felt across the school. The scheduling problems were so great and the principal's inability to understand the teachers' frustration so marked that, in at least one case, scheduling difficulties became the excuse for teachers to ignore fundamental curriculum and instruction issues.

The previous year's work on all-day kindergarten, particularly the work of the curriculum and facilities subcommittees, was only faintly echoed in this setting. While the district as a whole was committed to all-day kindergarten and developmentally appropriate practice, the translation of theory to practice at Calhoun was, at best, problematic. An extended morning kindergarten continues there, however, even though there has been no school-wide adjustment of schedules to allow the kindergarten teachers the concentrated time with their classes that had originally been planned, nor have there been curriculum and instructional changes in the kindergarten or elsewhere that would signal the emergence of an early childhood approach in the school.

A LOOK TO THE FUTURE

Four years later, Middle City is still without all-day kindergarten in any of its schools, but there is broad support for the program among parents and professionals throughout the district and there is hope that the financial constraints under which the district is operating will be eased enough to allow adoption of the plan advocated by the All-Day Kindergarten Task Force.

Was the effort to initiate all-day kindergarten a success in Middle City? In many ways, the answer is "yes, but . . . ." The will to change is there. The question becomes, "How long will it last?" As the time between the work of the All-Day Kindergarten Task Force and implementation of a district-wide program increases, the commitment and understanding forged in those five months of work will dissipate. Already members of the school board have left. So, too, have the superintendent and assistant superintendent. The children of the kindergarten parents who worked on the task force have moved on in school; their parents' sights are focused on new issues. It may be that the window of opportunity has closed. It is too soon to tell.

CHAPTER 6

Lessons from the Field

What took place in Rosedale and Middle City was not unusual for a substantive innovation, particularly one that involves early childhood. Early childhood innovations, probably more than any other type of change, challenge not only what Sarason (1982) calls the "regularities" of schools—habitual patterns of operation—but also the operative norms and beliefs that shape the climate and guide the activities of schools: The reach of early childhood innovations is both broad and deep, touching parents, teachers, administrators, and policy-makers and causing dissonance within and between each group. Both the efforts to initiate all-day kindergarten and the implementations of extended morning kindergarten programs in Rosedale and Middle City provide good illustrations of this point.

"TINKERING OF CONSEQUENCE"

All-day kindergarten constitutes a significant change in many school systems. It is, as Hills (1985) suggests, "tinkering of consequence." While it looks like a simple schedule change, its ramifications go far beyond scheduling, requiring adjustments in staffing, transportation, site selection, cost, and administration within schools, and adjustments of time, child care, and child-care arrangements on the part of parents. The same is true of extended morning kindergarten programs. As the accounts of those programs suggest, the expansion of the school day for an extended morning program may be as intrusive as all-day kindergarten on the overall program of the elementary school. Although problems of transportation, food, cost, administration, and parental concerns about length of day were quickly and easily addressed in both settings, the issue of teachers' schedules became a critical one.

In Rosedale, the scheduling issue focused on ensuring that the full-time kindergarten teacher had something to do in the afternoon, leading to the principal's limited call-back initiative. In Middle City, when the extended day kindergarten was implemented, the scheduling issue became a bone of contention between the principal and the kindergarten teachers on two fronts: coverage of the teachers' lunch hour, which was also the overlap time between the morning and afternoon kindergarten classes, and the scheduling of special enrichment activities to allow continuity in the kindergarten day. In both cases, the principals waded into the new programs without having done adequate initial planning with the teachers. The irony is that neither situation would have been problematic in an all-day kindergarten program.

All-day kindergarten, as these stories make clear, touches on deeply held beliefs about good mothering, parent involvement in schools, developmentally appropriate practice, and the status of early childhood education in schools.

The "Good" Mother

In Rosedale, the issue of good mothering, while never named as such, was ever present in the district's tug-of-war over the length of the kindergarten day. It was there in the very first meetings during the spring before the Ad Hoc Committee was formed and the extended morning program was begun. It was there in the final deliberations of the school board. It was heard in the board member's remark, "Kindergarten should be part with mommy and part with school." Time in school and program cost were the bargaining chips that represented the issue of good mothering in the deliberations between parents and policy-makers on the length of the kindergarten day. An extended morning program was an optimal compromise, offering additional time while preserving the appearance of the primacy of the home in the care and education of young children. No one chose to point out the obvious: that only one child in the Rosedale kindergarten went home every afternoon (the others all had some type of organized after-school activity planned for them), or that the purported savings of $4,739 in the cost of the extended morning program over an all-day kindergarten program was negligible in a multimillion dollar budget.

By their refusal to discuss the issue of child care, the "old Rosedale" members of the Ad Hoc Committee and the school board demonstrated indifference to the fact that societal and economic changes, even in that affluent suburb, had altered the experience of young families and their ability to provide for their children. The school board's acceptance of an after-school, child-care option financed largely by parents and its approval of the Ad Hoc Committee recommendation for the continuation of the extended morning program speak to the board members' beliefs about the roles of parents and the school in the care and education of young children: Good mothers stay home with their children; good schools provide education, *not* child care.

Parent Involvement in Schools

In early childhood education, parent involvement is a particularly important issue since parents' participation in and understanding of their child's experience is critical to the "success" of many early childhood programs. The younger the child, the more important is parent involvement.

In Rosedale, the issue of parent involvement, like the issue of good mothering, was never clearly articulated, but it was ever present in the daily interactions of teachers with other teachers and of teachers and administrators with parents. In the elementary school, it was fairly easy to distinguish parents from teachers in the following ways:

1. *Dress.* Teachers, even the kindergarten teachers, dressed professionally; parents, particularly kindergarten parents, often appeared at school dressed casually, with babies or young children in tow.
2. *Language.* Teachers spoke in jargon, "educationese," thus distancing themselves from parents. The clearest example of this during my year of observation was the use of the term "diagnostic screening." As late as the May school board meeting, there was still confusion on the part of parents and board members about its meaning.
3. *Use of the school building.* Teachers were comfortable in the school; parents were not. They had to stop in the office and get permission to go to their child's classroom. They frequently had an escort through the building. Parent volunteers signed in at the office. When parents and teachers met individually, as in a parent–teacher conference, and when they met in groups, as on back to school nights, the meetings generally took place in the classroom where parents

had to accommodate to child-sized furniture. There was no special place for parents to meet, so, for example, the locus of Ad Hoc Committee meetings changed to a different room in the elementary school each time the group met. It is interesting to note, too, that when the two kindergarten teachers were interviewed in the home of one of the Ad Hoc Committee members, they appeared to be insecure and out of place.

4. *Interactions.* Teachers rarely met with parents for other than official activities: back to school night, testing, parent–teacher conferences. Class mothers and other parent volunteers looked to the teachers for guidance with regard to their classroom activities. Teachers who called home had specific agendas, such as a needed signature, trip money, or difficulties with a child; they appeared as authorities to parents.

The relationships between parents and teachers in Rosedale are not unique to that setting; they are fairly typical of school districts around the country. There is a distance between teachers and parents that makes both groups appear somewhat defensive with each other and unable to really communicate about the matter of critical importance to both— the child that they share.

In Middle City, these differences were not obvious during the meetings of the Kindergarten Task Force. Because the task force meetings were held in the evening, both professionals and parents appeared in similar attire. For the most part, language and status were not issues that appeared to affect their interactions since they were meeting regularly in meeting rooms at the district office, not in the schools, and were preparing their reports together in subcommittees. There was, however, evidence from the parent involvement subcommittee's bimonthly reports that suggests that had the all-day kindergarten program in Middle City actually come into being, parent involvement in the schools might have surfaced as a critical issue for negotiation. These reports were prescriptive about the family's role in preparing children for school and in working with teachers to support learning at home. They appeared to be aimed at the low-SES, minority, and/or non-English-speaking parents who did not participate in the task force discussions, and they suggest another fairly typical pattern in schools: a gulf in understanding between the largely middle-class teachers and administrators who work in and manage schools and the growing number of low-income and minority families whose children use the public schools.

Staff Development and Teacher Initiative
in Early Childhood Practice

Teaching and curriculum that are developmentally appropriate for young children are qualitatively different from standard conceptions of teaching and learning in the elementary school. In Rosedale and Middle City, the all-day kindergarten planning committees acknowledged the differences. However, only the Middle City committee formed a plan for staff development designed to engage *elementary educators* in early childhood practice, and neither district provided the support to the kindergarten teachers who were developing and implementing extended morning programs that would have enabled them to engage in substantive curricular and instructional revision.

It could be argued that since both of these cases involved all-day kindergarten initiatives rather than implementations, planning for staff development was unnecessary. However, the research on change, particularly work by Berman and McLaughlin (1978), Fullan and Steigelbauer (1991), and Barth (1990), suggests that teachers' understanding and willingness to work with an innovation are critical to its successful implementation. Planning for staff development, then, becomes an essential part of the mobilization stage of change. As these cases suggest, staff development may be particularly important in early childhood innovations for both elementary and early childhood teachers to facilitate curricular integration, collegial interaction, and developmentally appropriate instruction.

In Rosedale, the fundamental differences between early childhood and elementary practice were largely ignored. Were an all-day kindergarten program to be implemented there, it is not clear whether there would be negotiation and compromise between early childhood and elementary educators. There was no effort to engage in staff development for kindergarten and primary faculties during the implementation of the extended morning kindergarten program.

Commitment to staff development for early childhood education was also questionable in the extended morning program in Middle City. Despite their participation in the All-Day Kindergarten Task Force the previous year, neither the principal nor the kindergarten teachers involved in the extended morning program sought to engage the elementary faculty in staff development focused on early childhood practice.

Furthermore, the early childhood educators on the scene during both of these extended morning kindergarten implementations—the full-time kindergarten teacher in Rosedale, and several of the kindergarten teachers in Middle City—did not model and advocate for specific early childhood practices, such as alternatives to standardized testing; close, supportive interaction with parents; and constructivist curricula that stress interactive play and "hands-on learning." This suggests that these teachers were not prepared to act as change agents for their early childhood programs. For them, it might have been useful to provide staff development focused on leadership, coupled with broad-reaching administrative support for their programs.

The Status of Early Childhood Education in Schools

Status refers to the relative importance of an individual, group, or organization vis-á-vis other individuals, groups, or organizations. There is ample evidence in the cases of Rosedale and Middle City to suggest that early childhood education did not enjoy high status in these school systems.

Positions of Kindergarten Teachers. To begin with, the kindergarten positions in both settings were regularly filled by elementary teachers who had little or no specific preparation for working with young children, thus suggesting perceptions of kindergarten teaching as being either not different from teaching at any other level of the elementary school or so simple as not to require special preparation. In either case, the unique skills and knowledge that mark excellent early childhood pedagogy appear to have been undervalued. A further indication of the low status of the kindergarten teachers was the fact that both kindergarten programs were separate and apart from the rest of the elementary school: Their schedules precluded interaction between the kindergarten and elementary school teachers during the school day.

Influence. In Rosedale, the kindergarten teacher was isolated, even insulated, from decision making. For five consecutive years, she alone had designed the kindergarten curriculum and trained elementary teachers for the kindergarten classes. With the all-day kindergarten proposal, she let the principal guide the initiative, plan the evaluation of the extended morning program (including the evaluation procedures), and argue for her position by proposing the limited call-back program. She was unaware that there had been a discussion between the school administrators and the teachers union regarding teacher representation on the Ad Hoc Committee. Neither she nor the principal, nor any other administrators, teachers, or parents, insisted on her active representation of an early childhood perspective in the district's deliberations on all-day kindergarten. When the principal announced her decision to retire, the kindergarten teacher reluctantly assumed an advocacy position but focused her energies entirely on the staffing problems of the extended morning program for the following year, thus ignoring the larger debate on all-day kindergarten and early childhood practice in the elementary school. It was the parents on the Ad Hoc Committee with experience in early childhood education and the director of a local nursery school, not the kindergarten teacher, who raised the alarm about the issue of inadequate and inappropriate staffing in the Ad Hoc Committee recommendations. It may be that as the only early childhood educator in the entire district, the kindergarten teacher felt unable and, therefore, unwilling to advocate for the substantive curricular and instructional change that all-day kindergarten could bring.

Like the kindergarten teacher in Rosedale, the teachers in Middle City engaged administrators in the initiative, but unlike their counterparts in Rosedale, these teachers were active participants throughout the all-day kindergarten discussion. Theirs was a broad-based initiative engaging parents, administrators, school board members, and teachers. Missing, however, from these discussions were key representatives from the elementary teachers' group, such as union leaders, whose advocacy of early childhood practices would carry weight in their schools. When the principal at the Calhoun School in Middle City initiated the extended morning program, it was clear that no one—not the principal himself, not the kindergarten and elementary teachers, not even the parents—saw this early childhood innovation as having an impact beyond the kindergarten.

Cost. In the end, neither all-day kindergarten initiative succeeded. Both were halted because of cost. How important was the cost factor? It was minimal in Rosedale. With the extended morning program, the district had already made most of the essential technical changes necessary for an all-day kindergarten. The problem there was not one of financial cost; it was an issue of political cost involving importance and beliefs. The new, young families who had initially supported the initiative were powerless to affect the school board's decision. After all, they were a minority in a district where only half the populace had children in the schools. "Old Rosedale" members of the Ad Hoc Committee, school board members, the superintendent—no one in a decision-making position felt that school-sponsored early childhood programs, other than kindergarten, were necessary for the children of this middle-class district. They did not want more emotional debate like that of the preceding year. All-day kindergarten wasn't that important.

In Middle City, the financial cost was important in the decision not to implement all-day kindergarten. The task force recommendations focused on creating an early childhood center in which the district's existing early childhood programs could be brought together with all-day kindergarten and with first and second grades. Without developing adequate space and completing a significant reorganization of the school system, the task force recommendation was not feasible.

In both Rosedale and Middle City, the apparently low status accorded early childhood education was a critical factor in the outcome of these initiatives. It should be no surprise to anyone that neither extended morning program has had curricular or instructional impact beyond the kindergarten. It is highly likely that without the dynamic support of the district office and the financial support of the school board, the all-day kindergarten initiative in Middle City will languish. Early childhood education in these and many other districts is not a primary concern among policy-makers.

MOBILIZATION

In many ways, the Middle City initiative can be judged successful. It is clear that the Rosedale initiative was not. The differences between the two are strongly related to the planning processes followed in these settings.

Developing a Sense of Mission

One of the very first things that the small group of kindergarten teachers in Middle City did was develop a mission statement to guide their appraisal of the kindergarten and their research and planning for all-day kindergarten. This is a critical step in most successful change efforts (Sarason, 1972). It enables participants to talk about their ideas and to reach a common understanding of their goal; it unites them in their endeavor; and it facilitates entry of new members to a change effort. With early childhood innovations, development of a mission statement is particularly important as a means of educating about the field. As the stories of Rosedale and Middle City demonstrate, parents, administrators, and many teachers often know little about the philosophy and practices of early childhood education.

The mission statement for the Middle City kindergarten was simple and straightforward.

A positive experience in kindergarten is the foundation for future learning. A good kindergarten nurtures a positive self-image by providing developmentally appropriate learning experiences that enable children to develop their minds and bodies.

It points clearly to the importance of the kindergarten experience, developmentally appropriate practice, and a "whole child" approach. The initial review of the kindergarten program, the development of a needs assessment, and many of the actions taken by the Kindergarten Task Force in Middle City were shaped by this initial understanding.

As these cases suggest, all-day kindergarten and other early childhood innovations can cause significant disruption in a school system. Embarking on an early childhood innovation should be undertaken with care and attention to the needs of the district and the school(s). The reasons for initiating the change are critical to its outcome, as both the cases of Middle City and Rosedale demonstrate.

As a means of addressing racial and ethnic imbalance and providing high-quality early childhood education for all of the district's children, all-day kindergarten fit into the long-range goals and needs of Middle City. As a result, the issue of its value to the middle-class children of the district that so concerned the associate superintendent at the beginning of the all-day kindergarten planning initiative actually received minimal attention. This change of focus from issues related to socio-economic status to issues related to good education for the young children of the district provides a subtle demonstration of the power of perspective (House, 1981) to shape action. In Middle City, Dr. Flowers's insistence on addressing the long-range goals and needs of the district turned the attention of the group toward the broader political issues of equity, good schooling, and quality early childhood education and away from the cultural perspective (House, 1981) demonstrated in issues such as belief in the importance of neighborhood schools, the value of early childhood education for middle-class children, and responsibility for child care—any of which initially had the potential to factionalize task force members.

A similar transformation did not take place in Rosedale. Without a clear commitment from the district office to an exploration of the issue of quality early childhood education and in the absence of district-wide goals and objectives that made all-day kindergarten seem both important and necessary, the school personnel and the parents never had the in-depth conversations with one another that produced the broad-based commitment that emerged in Middle City. Instead, they remained separate, their discussions shaped by beliefs that seemed irreconcilable: Among the members of the Ad Hoc Committee and the school board, the issue was good mothering; among the school personnel, it was job retention. There was no guiding vision here, no need for either group to adopt a broader perspective.

Defining Relationships

Along with development of a philosophy statement goes designing a system for working together. Like the federal constitution, Sarason (1972) suggests that a system that spells out relationships in anticipation of difficulties, both interpersonal and systemic, can, in the long run, ensure the successful implementation and institutionalization of a new program. In Middle City, there was such an understanding; in Rosedale, there was not. The differences in process and outcomes are remarkable.

From the very beginning, the district office in Middle City was involved in the all-day kindergarten initiative, first to help design the initiative, later to support and monitor it. From the beginning, it was understood that the decision regarding all-day kindergarten would be made by the school board in concert with the superintendent. Participation was sought from parents, early childhood and elementary teachers, administrators, community leaders, and the school board. The full range of information and services that the task force needed was made available, including consultant support. The process that the task force engaged in was designed to encourage interaction, dialogue, development of understanding, and commitment. The cohesiveness of the Middle City endeavor contrasts sharply with the balkanization that took place in Rosedale, where parents were at odds with professionals, the Ad Hoc Committee was competing with the school, and the district office and the school board were deeply involved in placating each faction while trying to maintain a "hands-off" policy.

Providing and Sharing Leadership

While the initiatives in Rosedale and Middle City began with kindergarten teachers, their management quickly changed hands. In Rosedale, the principal took over. In Middle City, it was the associate superintendent who initially guided the project and brought in consultants to shape and support it. Rosedale's effort was not successful; Middle City's holds promise. Both efforts speak to the complex nature of leadership in the change process.

Research by Berman and McLaughlin (1978), Fullan and Steigelbauer (1991), McLaughlin and Marsh (1978), and others tells us that it is essential that district office support be signaled from the beginning; that the principal be involved throughout; that the reasons for the change be widely understood; and that the day-to-day management of the change effort be handled by those who have an in-depth understanding of the innovation.

The actions of the principal in Rosedale over the year of study make it clear that she embraced the all-day kindergarten initiative for reasons quite different from those of the kindergarten teacher and that she did not have a deep understanding of early childhood practice. The associate superintendent in Middle City, by contrast, demonstrated commitment, understanding, and a willingness to cooperate closely with the early childhood teachers who were integral to the planning process.

The cohesiveness of the Middle City effort demonstrates not only broad-based support but also shared leadership—in this case, a willingness to work together toward a common goal by tapping the strengths of each member of the team. The planning process that shaped the task force's work was designed to promote trust, shared decision making, and broad commitment. The all-day kindergarten initiative was not an extra burden for an administrator, to be managed during an already busy day, as was the case for the principal in Rosedale; it was a district-wide endeavor that had its own space and time and guidance from a team of consultants whose focus was developing a plan for all-day kindergarten.

Using Change Agents: Insiders or Outsiders

The decision about whether to use a consultant depends largely on two factors: the nature of the innovation and the history of the setting. Many innovations are guided by "insiders," teachers or administrators who know both the innovation and the setting intimately and are thereby able to marshal the resources and establish the parameters necessary to ensure the innovation's success. Barbara Thornton's program for the gifted and talented is a good example. There are many innovations, however, in which "outsiders" are the more appropriate choice, as in Middle City, where Dr. Baxter and I were able to bring individuals together in ways and over tasks that might not have been as easily managed by insiders.

Sometimes, the history of the setting can be a good indicator of the efficacy of engaging a consultant. Dr. Baxter's long history of successful work with the Middle City school district was especially important. We were able to begin our work secure in the knowledge that we had the trust and support of the district office and a free hand in designing and implementing the planning process. By contrast, my work with the kindergarten teachers at Calhoun was problematic. There, a "helping teacher" was the consulting model that had been used most often. My every-three-week sessions with the teachers did not provide the daily support that was needed. Nor was there teacher and administrative support for the substantive changes in curriculum and teaching that the school's movement to an extended morning program had signaled.

Consultants cannot create systemic change. Given the right conditions—support, trust, time—they can help to create and maintain a climate in which it is nurtured.

IMPLEMENTATION

While neither district embarked on an all-day kindergarten program, the implementation of the extended morning program in each holds some lessons for management of new programs.

Leadership

In both settings, the principals were able to make changes that no one else could have managed. They tested the limits and found them permeable. In Rosedale, Barbara Thornton argued successfully for a limited call-back program even though it had the potential to cause a serious rift between the school board and the Ad Hoc Committee. In Middle City, the principal at Calhoun was able to implement an extended morning kindergarten program when district-wide efforts to lengthen the kindergarten day were on hold. Had these principals been better informed about early childhood practice and had they supported the extended morning kindergarten program for different reasons, it is likely that systemic rather than cosmetic change would have accompanied the implementation of these two programs.

Teacher leadership is also essential for the implementation of an innovation. Where there is a core of teachers who believe in, use, and model the innovation, others will try it. While there was a strong core of teacher-believers in the All-Day Kindergarten Task Force in Middle City, they were not part of the Calhoun extended morning program. As in Rosedale, the one kindergarten teacher who was well-versed in early childhood practice was either unable or unwilling to assume a leadership role. Thus, teacher leadership was virtually nonexistent in the implementation of these early childhood programs.

Management and Support

Management and support during implementation are aspects of leadership that reside mainly in the hands of principals and teachers. In Middle City, the teachers' preoccupation with the schedule and their inability to reach a constructive compromise with the principal made it impossible for them to move toward consideration of the content of their program. In Rosedale, the principal's focus on "hard data," coupled with the concern that she shared with the teachers about their positions in the future, precluded reassessment of the curriculum and restructuring of the relationships between the kindergarten and the primary grades.

In both settings, the teachers' responses to the additional time provided by the new schedule were minimal: Essentially, they gave their students more time to do what they had been doing with kindergartners prior to the extended morning programs. This is "co-optation": that response to change described by Berman and McLaughlin (1978) in which participants in an innovation make it look like they are using it, but in fact change nothing.

INSTITUTIONALIZATION

The extended morning kindergartens have continued in both Rosedale and Middle City. They are now integral parts of the elementary programs of both schools. But little has changed. Their integration into the fabric of these schools is an example of what Berman and McLaughlin (1978) call "pro forma continuation" (p. 16): They are established now as district policy; however, there is little perceptible difference in the conduct of instruction in the kindergarten classes or in the rest of the school.

Had the teachers and the principals in these two schools shared a vision, planned these programs together, and developed commitment to implementing early childhood practices, these extended morning kindergartens might have been the catalysts for significant change in the elementary schools: All-day kindergartens and other early childhood innovations might be in place and trumpeted as indicators of creative leadership in both districts. As it is, both extended morning kindergartens strongly resemble what was there before: They remain somewhat isolated in the elementary program, with their teachers on different schedules from other teachers in the building and their students doing work that is almost but not quite like that of the primary grades. Early childhood education has made little headway in either setting.

SUMMING UP

As these stories make clear, early childhood innovations, probably more than most others affecting schools, challenge not only long-standing traditions in schooling and instruction but also deeply held beliefs about child rearing and motherhood. For those who would bring early childhood programs into schools, there are numerous lessons here, the most obvious being

- The importance of a shared vision that is communicated early and understood broadly
- The need for a planning process that allows for questioning, interaction, and broad participation
- The critical role of leadership and support from the district office and school administrators
- The critical need for early childhood educators, whether insiders or outsiders, who can function as change agents, articulating the philosophy and theory that guide early childhood practice, serving as models for colleagues, and facilitating the practical discussions that must take place if early childhood practice is to take root in schools

Early childhood practice has the power to transform the elementary school. Whether it will depends on how early childhood programs are integrated in schools. Without the careful, inclusive planning that marked the process in Middle City, the chances of their resulting in more than cosmetic change are small. Without support, commitment, and informed leadership, it is unlikely that early childhood programs will occupy more than a marginal position in schools. Without a model of skilled practice provided by early childhood educators who are articulate and persuasive about the value of their approach, it is likely that early childhood practice will lose its distinctive character and come increasingly to resemble elementary education.

The efforts to initiate all-day kindergarten in Rosedale and Middle City speak volumes about the adjustments that must be made by parents, teachers, administrators, and policy-makers if early childhood programs are to be fully implemented in the schools. Change will be required in instruction throughout the elementary school, in administration of early childhood and elementary programs, in home–school–community relationships, and in professional relationships. It will require time and energy, negotiation and compromise, vision and commitment.

Part III

LOOKING AHEAD

CHAPTER 7

Early Childhood Education at a Crossroads

The movement of early childhood programs into schools places early childhood education at a crossroads: Early childhood innovations could be easily assimilated as technical changes—a few hours more of school, a younger group of students—thus losing their identity as programs specifically designed to meet the needs and abilities of young children; or, they could have a leavening influence on the structure of schools and the conduct of education. The choice, I believe, rests with early childhood educators, for there is little to suggest that schools themselves are open to or capable of initiating such change themselves. Many of the clues about the obstacles that must be overcome as well as the actions that should be taken are embedded in the stories of Rosedale and Middle City.

OBSTACLES TO OVERCOME

Beliefs About Early Childhood

To begin with, we must recognize that early childhood education touches on deeply held beliefs about the care and education of young children. Beliefs, as House (1981) points out and as the case of Rosedale demonstrates, are not easily changed. Issues must be redefined in such a way as to facilitate discussion and debate. The case of Middle City provides an apt demonstration of how this might be done. There the issue of all-day kindergarten as a viable curricular and instructional decision for the district was recast as part of the larger issue of how young children should be educated. Everyone—parents, teachers, administrators, policy-makers—had something to say about the education of young children. Early childhood educators were able to take a leading role in defining the parameters of the discussion and shaping its outcome—a recommendation that went far beyond anything anyone had anticipated at the beginning of the process.

We must also recognize that early childhood practice is not congruent with thinking about teaching and curriculum in most elementary schools. To adopt the child-centered, constructivist philosophy and methods of early childhood education requires that elementary school teachers, administrators, and parents revise their understandings of how children learn and of the role of schools in that process. Such deep, substantive change does not come quickly or easily. It requires vision, commitment, sustained support, and leadership.

Perceptions of the Field

A second obstacle that we must confront is that early childhood education is not widely recognized as a distinct and well-articulated field of education. It is perceived as "women's work," with concomitant low status and low pay. Often separated from the rest of the elementary school by schedule, the age of the children involved, and the different physical settings they require, early childhood programs are out of the mainstream of schools, their students perceived as "cute," their curriculum and teaching perceived as lacking in substance—not real teaching.

These misperceptions are enacted in administrative decisions such as the assignment of upper-grade teachers to the kindergarten, as happened in Rosedale, or the transfer of poorly performing teachers to the kindergarten and lower grades. They figure in elementary teachers' resistance to such early childhood practices as hands-on math and science, whole language, and authentic assessment. They are embedded in policy-makers' decisions about the allocation of resources in schools: Invariably, as the cases of both Rosedale and Middle City suggest, early childhood programs are seen as less important than programs in secondary schools. Arguments that strong early childhood programs can result in long-term savings, as remedial and other support expenditures are reduced, fall on deaf ears in middle-class school districts like Rosedale.

A Lack of Models

Rarely do early childhood programs function as catalysts for change in schools. Most often, they are changed and transformed by the school environment, becoming increasingly like traditional elementary programs with an emphasis on paper and pencil work, reading, and whole group instruction. This may be because there are few visions of settings in which developmentally appropriate practices thrive. For inspiration, one can turn to descriptions of teachers' at work in books like Lucy Calkins's *The Art of Teaching Writing* (1986), Eleanor Duckworth's *The Having of Wonderful Ideas* (1987), Doris Fromberg's *The Full-Day Kindergarten* (1987), Vivian Gussen Paley's *Wally's Stories* (1981), and Sylvia Ashton-Warner's *Teacher* (1963). But real life examples that teachers, administrators, and policy-makers can turn to for study and experiential learning are even more rare. There are the British Infant Schools, and there is Montessori's work and some of the very good schools that follow her method. Currently, the material coming out on Reggio Emilia in Italy (see New, 1990) holds promise. None of these programs, however, have been easily assimilated into public school settings. For that, we must turn to the High Scope programs (Schweinhart, Weikart, & Larner, 1986; Schweinhart & Weikart, 1988), the BEEP Program in Brookline (Hauser-Cram et al., 1991), Deborah Meier's work at the Central Park East Elementary School, the early childhood programs in Buffalo that are described by Haskins and Alessi (1989), and other small programs scattered across the country. Where such programs have had a significant impact on curriculum and teaching in the elementary school (see Jarvis & Molnar, 1986) or on the allocation of resources in school systems (see Haskins & Alessi, 1989), they hold valuable lessons for early childhood educators.

The Problem of Preparation for the Field

Professional preparation for the field is a double-edged sword. On one side are the large number of early childhood personnel who have not had professional preparation: While their work may be exemplary, issues of certification and licensure prevent them from working in the schools as teachers. On the other side are those who seek professional preparation only to find that there are very few early childhood preservice programs and that certification and licensure specific to early childhood education are virtually nonexistent. By and large, new early childhood teachers prepare for the field of elementary education, taking some early childhood courses and having one or two field experiences in early childhood settings. Their teaching certification extends from nursery school through sixth grade; their chances of finding good paying teaching positions in pre-kindergarten programs are few.

A Lack of Leadership

The cases of Rosedale and Middle City make it clear that many early childhood educators are ill-prepared to be change agents and advocates for their programs in schools. Nor are these roles generally expected of them. In many instances, early childhood teachers are "co-opted" by the system: Like the kindergarten teacher in Rosedale, they find themselves without peer support for the uncomplicated, direct, and highly interactive work that is customary in early childhood centers. As both extended morning programs demonstrate, it is difficult for early childhood teachers in public schools to challenge the practice of their elementary colleagues or to assume a voice in policy-making. To "fit in," they adopt the instructional practices, the dress, the jargon, and the habits of their elementary colleagues. Inevitably, they distance themselves from the parents, who, in early childhood settings, are not only their primary sources of support but also their partners in the education of young children.

TAKING ACTION

To effect change in the schools, early childhood educators have available to them the broad range of resources that have been the hallmark and strength of this field—belief in the child's ability to learn, commitment to developmentally appropriate practice, strong home–school relationships, and a tradition of collegiality and interaction among professionals. As schools seek to "re-invent" (Meier, 1992) and "re-structure" (Cohen, 1987) themselves, early childhood educators have the potential to assume a strong leadership role, for no other group of educators has the skills and knowledge bred of experience that are needed to effect the substantive changes ahead for schools in the process of restructuring: There is a wealth of strong, viable early childhood programs that could serve as models of school-based management, shared decision making, collegial interaction, community involvement in education, cooperative learning, constructivist teaching, and more.

Taking a leadership role will require significant change within the field itself on a variety of fronts, from local to national, and with a variety of initiatives, including teacher preparation, inservice training, curriculum revision, organizational management, licensure, and advocacy. Early childhood educators cannot stay on the sidelines hoping that the winds of change will pass gently over the field. As early childhood programs enter the mainstream, early childhood educators should be actively working to preserve the integrity of their programs and the field and, at the same time, seeking to reshape the programs that their students will move into. In doing so, they are bound to run into the inertia within the field and within schools that Herzog (1964) described when he wrote that "most approaches to the concept of change fail to recognize that most people are attached to whatever they are currently doing because they believe in the value of it, not because they are resistant to change" (p. 3). Standardized testing, tracking, graded classrooms, teachers working in isolation, whole group instruction, basal reading approaches, workbook and drill activities—these will not go away because early childhood educators argue against them as being developmentally inappropriate. They represent deeply held beliefs about learning, teaching, and the role of schools in society. Early childhood teachers and administrators should be prepared to articulate the rationales of their programs and to advocate for developmentally appropriate practice, not just because it is good and appropriate for young children but because, in the context of modern learning theory, it is logical for all children.

The lessons of these case studies can help, but they are not enough. Greater familiarity with theory and research on change is also required of early childhood educators as they assume a more assertive stance in education. Early childhood educators must be prepared to reframe the debate, to focus, as the planners in Middle City did, on the issue of good education. They must be willing to confront inequities in funding and resource allocation for their programs and inequities in schooling that are the outgrowth of prejudice and intolerance. For support, they will need to draw on the strengths of the field's traditional constituencies: parents, communities, and professionals in other service fields. There is no limit to the transformation that could take place if these groups united as one voice calling for new and better ways of educating not only young children but all of the nation's children.

References

ASCD Early Childhood Education Policy Panel. (1988). Analysis of issues concerning public school involvement in early childhood education. In C. Warger (Ed.), *A resource guide to public school early childhood programs* (pp. 99–115). Alexandria, VA: Association for Supervision and Curriculum Development.

Ashton-Warner, S. (1963). *Teacher.* New York: Simon & Schuster.

Bailey, W. J., & Neale, D. C. (1980). Teachers and school improvement. *The Educational Forum, 14,* 69–76.

Barth, R. (1990). *Improving schools from within.* San Francisco: Jossey-Bass.

Beckner, T. L., & others. (1979). *A study of the relationship of kindergarten class size, length and schedule of the kindergarten day, and teacher self-concept to school success.* (ERIC Document Reproduction Service No. ED 165 891)

Berman, P. B., & McLaughlin, M. W. (1978). Implementing and sustaining innovations. In *Federal programs supporting educational change: Vol. 8* (R-1589/8-HEW). Santa Monica, CA: Rand.

Berrueta-Clement, J., Schweinhart, L., Barnett, W., Epstein, A., & Weikart, D. (1984). *Changed lives.* Ypsilanti, MI: High/Scope Press.

Bloom, B. B. (1964). *Stability and change in human characteristics.* New York: Wiley.

Boehm, A. E. (1970). *The Boehm test of basic concepts.* New York: Psychological Corp.

Bowman, B. (1991). Educating language minority children: Challenges and opportunities. In S. L. Kagan (Ed.), *The care and education of America's young children: Obstacles and opportunities. Nineteenth yearbook of the National Society for the Study of Education* (pp. 17–29). Chicago: University of Chicago Press.

Bredekamp, S., & Shepard, L. (1989, March). How best to protect children from inappropriate school expectations, practices, and policies. *Young Children, 44*(3), 14–24.

Brigance, A. H. (1982). *Brigance K and 1 screen for kindergarten and first grade.* North Billerica, MA: Curriculum Associates.

Bruner, J. (1960). *The process of education.* Cambridge, MA: Harvard University Press.

Burrello, L. C., & Orbaugh, T. (1982). Reducing the discrepancy between the known and the unknown in inservice education. *Phi Delta Kappan, 63*, 385–388.

Caldwell, B. M. (1989, June). All-day kindergarten—Assumption, precautions, and overgeneralizations. *Early Childhood Research Quarterly, 4*(2), 261–266.

Caldwell, B. M. (1991). Continuity in the early years: Transitions between grades and systems. In S. L. Kagan (Ed.), *The care and education of America's young children: Obstacles and opportunities. Nineteenth yearbook of the National Society for the Study of Education* (pp. 69–90). Chicago: University of Chicago Press.

Calkins, L. M. (1986). *The art of teaching writing.* Portsmouth, NH: Heinemann.

Campbell, B. D. (1987). From national debate to national responsibility. In S. L. Kagan & E. F. Zigler (Eds.), *Early schooling: The national debate* (pp. 65–82). New Haven, CT: Yale University Press.

Caruso, D., & Detterman, K. (1982). Intelligence research and social policy. *Phi Delta Kappan, 63*, 183–186.

Chovinsky, M. (1982). *Preprimary enrollment—1980.* Washington, DC: National Center for Education Statistics.

Clark, A. M. (1984). Early experience and cognitive development. In E. W. Gordon (Ed.), *Review of research in education II* (pp. 125–161). Washington, DC: American Educational Research Association.

Clark, D., & Guba, E. (1965). *An examination of potential change roles in education.* Columbus: Ohio State University.

Cohen, M. (1987). *Restructuring the educational system: Agenda for the '90s.* Washington, DC: National Governors' Association.

Comer, J. P. (1980). *School power: Implications of an intervention project.* New York: Free Press.

Comer, J. P. (1989). Racism and the education of young children. In F. O'C. Rust & L. R. Williams (Eds.), *The care and education of young children: Expanding contexts, sharpening focus* (pp. 26–38). New York: Teachers College Press.

Consortium for Longitudinal Studies. (1983). *As the twig is bent . . . Lasting effects of preschool programs.* Hillsdale, NJ: Lawrence Erlbaum Associates.

Cotton, K., & Conklin, N. F. (1989, January). *Research on early childhood education. Topical synthesis #3: School improvement series.* Portland, OR: The Northwest Regional Educational Laboratory.

Cox, P. L., & Havelock, R. G. (1982). *External facilitators and their role in the improvement of practice.* Paper presented at the annual meeting of the American Educational Research Association, New York.

CTBS/McGraw-Hill. (1985). *California achievement tests.* New York: McGraw-Hill.

Cummins, J. (1986). Empowering minority students: A framework for intervention. *Harvard Educational Review, 56*(1), 18–36.

Deal, T. E. (1990). Reframing reform. *Educational Leadership, 47*(8), 6–12.

Duckworth, E. (1987). *"The having of wonderful ideas" and other essays on teaching and learning.* New York: Teachers College Press.

Edelman, M. W. (1989). Economic issues related to child care and early childhood education. In F. O'C. Rust & L. R. Williams (Eds.), *The care and education of young children: Expanding contexts, sharpening focus* (pp. 6–15). New York: Teachers College Press.

Elkind, D. (1981). *The hurried child.* Reading, MA: Addison-Wesley.

Elkind, D. (1986). Formal education and early childhood education: An essential difference. *Phi Delta Kappan, 67,* 631–636.

Elkind, D. (1987). Early childhood education on its own terms. In S. L. Kagan & E. F. Zigler (Eds.), *Early schooling: The national debate* (pp. 98–115). New Haven, CT: Yale University Press.

Elkind, D. (1991). Developmentally appropriate practice: A case study of educational inertia. In S. L. Kagan (Ed.), *The care and education of America's young children: Obstacles and opportunities. Nineteenth yearbook of the National Society for the Study of Education* (pp. 1–16). Chicago: University of Chicago Press.

Farrar, E., DeSanctis, J. E., & Cohen, D. K. (1981). *Views from below: Implementation research in education.* Cambridge, MA: The Huron Institute.

Festinger, L., & Katz, D. (Eds.). (1953). *Research methods in the behavioral sciences.* New York: Holt, Rinehart & Winston.

Fromberg, D. P. (1987). *The full-day kindergarten.* New York: Teachers College Press.

Fromberg, D. P. (1989). Kindergarten: Current circumstances affecting curriculum. In F. O'C. Rust & L. R. Williams (Eds.), *The care and education of young children: Expanding contexts, sharpening focus* (pp. 56–67). New York: Teachers College Press.

Fullan, M. G., Bennett, B., & Rolheiser-Bennett, C. (1990). Linking classroom and school improvement. *Educational Leadership, 47*(8), 13–19.

Fullan, M., & Steigelbauer, S. (1991). *The new meaning of educational change.* New York: Teachers College Press.

Galinsky, E. (1991). The private sector as a partner in early care and education. In S. L. Kagan (Ed.), *The care and education of America's young children: Obstacles and opportunities. Nineteenth yearbook of the National Society for the Study of Education* (pp. 131–153). Chicago: University of Chicago Press.

Geertz, C. (1973). Thick description: Toward an interpretive theory of culture. In C. Geertz (Ed.), *The interpretation of cultures* (pp. 3–30). New York: Basic Books.

Geertz, C. (1983). Blurred genres: The refiguration of social thought. In C. Geertz (Ed.), *Local knowledge* (pp. 19–35). New York: Basic Books.

Geertz, C. (1984). From the native's point of view: On the nature of anthropological understanding. In R. Shweder & R. Levine (Eds.), *Culture theory* (pp. 123–136). New York: Cambridge University Press.

Goffin, S. G. (1989, June). Developing a research agenda for early childhood education: What can be learned from the research on teaching? *Early Childhood Research Quarterly, 4*(2), 187–204.

Goffin, S. G. (1992). Challenging the status quo: Serving as critical change agents. In S. G. Goffin & D. A. Stegelin (Eds.), *Changing kindergartens—Four success stories* (pp. 99–108). Washington, DC: National Association for the Education of Young Children.

Goffin, S. G., & Stegelin, D. A. (Eds.). (1992). *Changing kindergartens—Four success stories.* Washington, DC: National Association for the Education of Young Children.

Goldenberg, C., & Gallimore, R. (1991, November). Local knowledge, research knowledge, and educational change: A case study of early Spanish reading improvement. *Educational Researcher, 20*(8), 2–14.

Gornowich, D. J., & others. (1974). *A school district looks at an alternative to half-day, every day kindergarten programs.* (ERIC Document Reproduction Service No. ED 107 347)

Graham, P. A. (1992). *S. O. S.: Sustain our schools.* Cambridge, MA: Harvard University Press.

Grover, S. P. (1990). The approach of a school system. In C. Kamii (Ed.), *Achievement testing in the early grades: The games grown-ups play* (pp. 49–59). Washington, DC: National Association for the Education of Young Children.

Grubb, W. N. (1991). Choosing wisely for children: Policy options for early childhood programs. In S. L. Kagan (Ed.), *The care and education of America's young children: Obstacles and opportunities. Nineteenth yearbook of the National Society for the Study of Education* (pp. 214–236). Chicago: University of Chicago Press.

Gullo, D. F., Bersani, C., Clements, D., & Bayless, K. M. (1986). A comparative study of all-day, alternate-day, and half-day kindergarten schedules: Effects on achievement and classroom social behaviors. *Journal of Research in Childhood Education, 1*(1), 87–94.

Haskins, G. P., & Alessi, S. J., Jr. (1989). An early childhood center developmental model for public school settings. In F. O'C. Rust & L. R. Williams (Eds.), *The care and education of young children: Expanding contexts, sharpening focus* (pp. 79–97). New York: Teachers College Press.

Hatcher, B., & Schmidt, V. (1980, September–October). Half-day vs. full-day kindergarten programs. *Childhood Education, 57,* 14–17.

Hauser-Cram, P., Pierson, D. E., Walker, D. K., & Tivnan, T. (1991). *Early education in the public schools: Lessons from a comprehensive birth-kindergarten program.* San Francisco: Jossey-Bass.

Heath, S. B. (1983). *Ways with words: Language, life, and work in communities and classrooms.* Cambridge: Cambridge University Press.

Herzog, J. D. (1964). Viewing the issues from the perspective of an R & D center. In D. D. Bushnell, R. S. Freeman, & M. Richland (Eds.), *Proceedings of the conference on the implementation of educational innovations* (pp. 3–8). Santa Monica, CA: Systems Development Corp.

Hiebert, E. H. (1988, November). The role of literacy experiences in early childhood programs. *The Elementary School Journal, 89*(2), 161–171.

Hilliard, A. G., III. (1991). Equity, access, and segregation. In S. L. Kagan (Ed.), *The care and education of America's young children: Obstacles and opportunities. Nineteenth yearbook of the National Society for the Study of Education* (pp. 199–213). Chicago: University of Chicago Press.

Hills, T. W. (1985). *All-day kindergarten: Resources for decision making.* Trenton: New Jersey State Department of Education, Division of General Academic Education. (ERIC Document Reproduction Service No. ED 287 603)

Hoegl, J. (1985). *Effectiveness of early childhood programs: A review of research.* Springfield: Illinois Board of Education, Department of Planning, Research, and Evaluation. (ERIC Document Reproduction Service No. ED 260 825)

House, E. R. (1981). Three perspectives on innovation: Technological, political, and cultural. In R. Lehming & M. Kane (Eds.), *Improving schools: Using what we know* (pp. 17–41). Beverly Hills, CA: Sage.

Ianni, F. A. J. (1972). *A family business.* New York: Russell Sage Foundation.

Ianni, F. A. J. (1977). Field research and educational administration. *UCEA Review, 17*(2), 10–13.

Jarvis, C. H., & Molnar, J. (1986). Getting started. *All-day kindergarten program: Classroom implementation.* New York: New York Public Schools Office of Educational Assessment. (ERIC Document Reproduction Service No. ED 289 610)

Johnson, J. M. (1975). *Doing field research.* New York: Free Press.

Kagan, S. L., & Zigler, E. F. (Eds.). (1987). *Early schooling: The national debate.* New Haven, CT: Yale University Press.

Kahn, A. J., & Kamerman, S. B. (1987). *Child care: Facing the hard choices.* Dover, MA: Auburn House.

Kamii, C. (Ed.). (1990). *Achievement testing in the early grades: The games grown-ups play*. Washington, DC: National Association for the Education of Young Children.

Karweit, N. (1988, November). Quality and quantity of learning time in preprimary programs. *The Elementary School Journal, 89*(2), 119–133.

Katz, D., & Kahn, R. (1975). Organizational change. In J. V. Baldridge & T. E. Deal (Eds.), *Managing change in educational organizations* (pp. 35–74). Berkeley, CA: McCutchan.

Katz, L. G. (1987). *Current issues in early childhood education*. Champaign, IL: ERIC Clearinghouse on Early Childhood Education. (ERIC Document Reproduction Service No. ED 281 908)

Katz, L. G. (1991). Pedagogical issues in early childhood education. In S. L. Kagan (Ed.), *The care and education of America's young children: Obstacles and opportunities. Nineteenth yearbook of the National Society for the Study of Education* (pp. 50–68). Chicago: University of Chicago Press.

Katz, L. G., & Chard, S. C. (1989). *Engaging children's minds: The project approach*. Norwood, NJ: Ablex.

Kluckhohn, F. R. (1940). The participant observer technique in small communities. *American Journal of Sociology, 46*, 331–343.

Lazar, I., & Darlington, R. (1982). Lasting effects of early education: A report from the Consortium for Longitudinal Studies. *Monographs of the Society for Research in Child Development, 47*(2–3, Serial No. 195).

Lazarson, M. (1988). Historical tensions/future opportunities. In L. R. Williams & D. P. Fromberg (Eds.), *The proceedings of: Defining the field of early childhood education. An invitational symposium* (pp. 21–40). Charlottesville, VA: The W. Alton Jones Foundation.

Lewin, K. (1961). Quasi stationary social equilibria and the problem of permanent change. In W. G. Bennis, K. D. Benne, & R. Chin (Eds.), *The planning of change* (2nd ed.) (pp. 235–238). New York: Holt, Rinehart, & Winston.

Lewis, K. S., & Miles, M. B. (1990). *Improving the urban high school: What works and why*. New York: Teachers College Press.

Lieberman, A., & Shiman, D. A. (1972). The stages of change in elementary school settings. In C. M. Culver & G. J. Hoban (Eds.), *The power to change: Issues for the innovative educator* (pp. 51–69). New York: McGraw-Hill.

Lindbloom, C. E. (1959). The science of "muddling through." *Public Administration Review, 19*, 79–88.

Loucks, S. F., & Cox, P. L. (1982). *School district personnel: A crucial role in school improvement efforts*. Paper presented at the annual meeting of the American Educational Research Association, New York.

Magid, R. Y. (1989). The consequences of employer involvement in child care. In F. O'C. Rust & L. R. Williams (Eds.), *The care and education of young children: Expanding contexts, sharpening focus* (pp. 98–107). New York: Teachers College Press.

Maguire, L. (1971). *Observations and analysis of the literature on change.* Philadelphia: Research for Better Schools.

May, L. (1992). Developing appropriate practices in the kindergarten: A district-level perspective. In S. G. Goffin & D. A. Stegelin (Eds.), *Changing kindergartens—Four success stories* (pp. 51–72). Washington, DC: National Association for the Education of Young Children.

McCall, G. J., & Simon, J. L. (1969). *Issues in participant observation: Text and reader.* Reading, MA: Addison-Wesley.

McLaughlin, M. W., & Marsh, D. D. (1978). Staff development and school change. *Teachers College Record, 80,* 69–94.

Meier, D. (1992). Reinventing schools. *Teachers College Record, 93*(4), 594–609.

Miel, A. (1946). *Changing the school curriculum.* New York: Appleton-Century.

Mooney, N. J. (1992). Coming to know: A principal's story. In S. G. Goffin & D. A. Stegelin (Eds.), *Changing kindergartens—Four success stories* (pp. 29–50). Washington, DC: National Association for the Education of Young Children.

Moore, E. K. (1987). Child care in the public schools: Public accountability and the black child. In S. L. Kagan & E. F. Zigler (Eds.), *Early schooling: The national debate* (pp. 83–97). New Haven, CT: Yale University Press.

Morgan-Worsham, D. (1990). The dilemma for principals. In C. Kamii (Ed.), *Achievement testing in the early grades: The games grown-ups play* (pp. 61–80). Washington, DC: National Association for the Education of Young Children.

Moss, M. (1979). *Test of basic experiences 2.* Monterey, CA: CTB/McGraw-Hill.

Murawski, E. L. (1992). Changing kindergartens: Teachers as change agents. In S. G. Goffin & D. A. Stegelin (Eds.), *Changing kindergartens—Four success stories* (pp. 13–28). Washington, DC: National Association for the Education of Young Children.

Naron, N. K. (1981). The need for full-day kindergarten. *Educational Leadership, 38,* 306–309.

National Association for the Education of Young Children. (1986, September). Position statement on developmentally appropriate practice in early childhood programs. *Young Children, 41*(6), 3–20.

National Association for the Education of Young Children. (1988, March).

Position statement on standardized testing of young children 3 through 8 years of age. *Young Children, 44*(3), 42–47.

National Commission on Excellence in Education. (1983). *A nation at risk.* Washington, DC: U.S. Department of Education.

New, R. (1990). Excellent early education: A city in Italy has it. *Young Children, 45*(6), 4–10.

Nieman, R. H., & Gastright, J. F. (1981). *The long term effects of ESEA Title I preschool and all-day kindergarten: An eight year follow-up study.* Cincinnati, OH: Cincinnati Public Schools. (ERIC Document Reproduction Service No. ED 198 949)

Oelerich, M. L. (1979). *Kindergarten: All day every day.* (ERIC Document Reproduction Service No. ED 179 282)

Olsen, D., & Zigler, E. (1989, June). An assessment of the all day kindergarten movement. *Early Childhood Research Quarterly, 4*(2),167–186.

Paley, V. G. (1981). *Wally's stories—Conversations in the kindergarten.* Cambridge, MA: Harvard University Press.

Peck, J. T., McCaig, G., & Sapp, M. E. (1988). *Kindergarten policies: What is best for children?* Washington, DC: National Association for the Education of Young Children.

Perrone, V. (1990). How did we get here? In C. Kamii (Ed.), *Achievement testing in the early grades: The games grown-ups play* (pp. 1–13). Washington, DC: National Association for the Education of Young Children.

Peskin, M. (1988). *Are social and economic changes in family patterns dictating the frequency and curriculum of all-day kindergarten?* (ERIC Document Reproduction Service No. ED 293 647)

Piaget, J. (1950). *The psychology of intelligence.* London: Rutledge & Kegan Paul.

Popkewitz, T. S. (1982). *The myth of educational reform.* Madison: University of Wisconsin.

Post, D. (1992). Through Joshua Gap: Curricular control and the constructed community. *Teachers College Record, 93*(4), 673–696.

Rauh, P. S. (1978). Helping teacher: A model for staff development. *Teachers College Record, 80,* 157–171.

Rust, F. O'C. (1982). *A review of research on all day kindergarten.* Hartford, CT: Department of Education.

Rust, F. O'C. (1984). *Implementation of an extended morning kindergarten: A case study of an educational innovation.* Unpublished doctoral dissertation, Teachers College, Columbia University.

Rust, F. O'C. (1989). Early childhood in public education: Managing change in a changing field. In F. O'C. Rust & L. R. Williams (Eds.), *The care and education of young children: Expanding contexts and sharpening focus* (pp. 116–128). New York: Teachers College Press.

Rust, F. O'C., & Williams, L. R. (Eds.). (1989). *The care and education of young children: Expanding contexts, sharpening focus.* New York: Teachers College Press.

Sarason, S. B. (1972). *The creation of settings and the future societies.* Washington, DC: Jossey-Bass.

Sarason, S. B. (1982). *The culture of the school and the problem of change* (2nd ed.). Boston: Allyn & Bacon.

Sarason, S. B. (1987). Policy, implementation, and the problem of change. In S. L. Kagan & E. F. Zigler (Eds.), *Early schooling: The national debate* (pp. 116–126). New Haven, CT: Yale University Press.

Schorr, L. B. (1988). *Within our reach: Breaking the cycle of disadvantage.* New York: Doubleday.

Schorr, L. B. (1989). Early interventions aimed at reducing intergenerational disadvantage: The new social policy. In F. O'C. Rust & L. R. Williams (Eds.), *The care and education of young children: Expanding contexts, sharpening focus* (pp. 26–38). New York: Teachers College Press.

Schultz, T., & Lombardi, J. (1989). Right from the start: A report on the NASBE Task Force on Early Childhood Education. *Young Children, 44,* 6–10.

Schwartz, M. S., & Schwartz, C. G. (1955). Problems in participant observation. *American Journal of Sociology, 60,* 343–354.

Schweinhart, L. J., & Weikart, D. P. (1988, November). Education for young children living in poverty: Child-initiated learning or teacher directed instruction? *The Elementary School Journal, 89*(2), 213–225.

Schweinhart, L. J., Weikart, D. P., & Larner, M. B. (1986). Consequences of three preschool models through age 15. *Early Childhood Research Quarterly, 1,* 15–45.

Sergiovanni, T. J. (1990). Adding value to leadership gets extraordinary results. *Educational Leadership, 47*(8), 23–27.

Shanker, A. (1987). The case for public school sponsorship of early childhood education revisited. In S. L. Kagan & E. F. Zigler (Eds.), *Early schooling: The national debate* (pp. 45–64). New Haven, CT: Yale University Press.

Shepard, L. A., & Smith, M. L. (1988, November). Escalating academic demand in kindergarten: Counterproductive policies. *The Elementary School Journal, 89*(2), 135–145.

Silvern, S. B. (1988, November). Continuity and discontinuity between home and early childhood education environments. *The Elementary School Journal, 89*(2), 147–160.

Smith, L. M., & Keith, P. M. (1971). *Anatomy of educational innovation. An organizational analysis of an elementary school.* New York: Wiley.

Spodek, B. (1988, November). Conceptualizing today's kindergarten curriculum. In *The Elementary School Journal, 89*(2), 203–211.

Spodek, B. (1991). Early childhood teacher training: Linking theory and practice. In S. L. Kagan (Ed.), *The care and education of America's young children: Obstacles and opportunities. Nineteenth yearbook of the National Society for the Study of Education* (pp. 110–130). Chicago: University of Chicago Press.

Stegelin, D. A. (1992). Kindergarten education: Current policy and practice. In S. G. Goffin & D. A. Stegelin (Eds.), *Changing kindergartens—Four success stories* (pp. 1–11). Washington, DC: National Association for the Education of Young Children.

Strauss, A. L. (1980). *Fieldwork, theoretical sampling and educational research.* Unpublished paper.

Strauss, A. L., Schatzman, I., Bucher, R., Erlich, D., & Sabshin, M. (1969). The process of field work. In G. J. McCall & J. L. Simon (Eds.), *Issues in participant observation* (pp. 24–26). Reading, MA: Addison-Wesley.

Suransky, V. P. (1982). *The erosion of childhood.* Chicago: University of Chicago Press.

Vidich, A. J. (1969). Participant observation and the collection and interpretation of data. In G. J. McCall & J. L. Simon (Eds.), *Issues in participant observation* (pp. 78–87). Reading, MA: Addison-Wesley.

Warger, C. (Ed.). (1988). *A resource guide to public school early childhood programs.* Alexandria, VA: Association for Supervision and Curriculum Development.

Weick, C. E. (1982). Administering change in loosely coupled schools. *Phi Delta Kappan, 63,* 673–676.

Weikart, D. P. (1987). Curriculum quality in early education. In S. L. Kagan & E. F. Zigler (Eds.), *Early schooling: The national debate* (pp. 168–189). New Haven, CT: Yale University Press.

Winn, M. (1983). *Children without childhood.* New York: Penguin.

Wolcott, H. F. (1977). *Teachers vs. technocrats.* Eugene: Center for Educational Policy and Management, University of Oregon.

Zelditch, M., Jr. (1962). Some methodological problems of field studies. *American Journal of Sociology, 67,* 566–576.

Zigler, E. F. (1987). Formal schooling for four-year-olds? No. In S. L. Kagan & E. F. Zigler (Eds.), *Early schooling: The national debate* (pp. 27–44). New Haven, CT: Yale University Press.

Zigler, E. F. (1991). Using research to inform policy: The case of early intervention. In S. L. Kagan (Ed.), *The care and education of America's young children: Obstacles and opportunities. Nineteenth yearbook of the National Society for the Study of Education* (pp. 154–172). Chicago: University of Chicago Press.

Index

About the Author

Frances O'Connell Rust is associate professor and coordinator of the Undergraduate Elementary Education Program in the Department of Teaching and Learning at New York University. She received both her undergraduate degree in English Literature and a Masters in Teaching from Manhattanville College and her Masters in Education and Doctoral degrees from Teachers College, Columbia University. Prior to her doctoral work, she was a preschool teacher/director in open classroom settings that she founded and developed. Before joining New York University, Frances Rust served as Associate Director of the Preservice Program at Teachers College, Columbia University; Director of the Department of Teacher Education at Manhattanville College; and Chair of the Department of Curriculum and Teaching at Hofstra University. Her research interests include teacher education, teacher beliefs, instructional supervision, and educational innovation. Her dissertation, *Implementation of an Extended Morning Kindergarten: A Case Study of an Educational Innovation*, won the 1984 AERA outstanding dissertation award for empirical research. Her most recent book is *The Care and Education of Young Children: Expanding Contexts, Sharpening Focus* (edited with Leslie Williams).